DEVELOPING
A CHRIST-CENTERED CHURCH

HENRY & RICHARD BLACKABY

Henry and Richard have captured in this book what I first saw lived out as a brand new Christian in Saskatoon, Saskatchewan. The victorious church led by Christ Himself who believes no God given mission or task is too big for it. The church is invigorated and energized by our Lord to give itself away for the Kingdom of God. If taken seriously the God perspective in this book could revive any church.

> – GERRY TAILLON, Retired National Ministry Leader, Canadian National Baptist Convention

As a boy growing up in Saskatchewan, I had the joy of experiencing first-hand what an all-powerful King can do through a pastor and a people who lived Kingdom first. It is my prayer that church leaders in plateaued and declining churches will read this book and then courageously follow the example of Henry Blackaby and Faith Baptist Church. Any church that will put the Kingdom of God before ecclesiastical self-interest will find themselves in the flow of God's gracious and redemptive mission. May the selfless pursuit contained in these pages change the trajectory of scores of churches that are now sadly destined for extinction.

> – JEFF CHRISTOPHERSON, National Ministry Leader of Canadian National Baptist Convention NAMB; author, Kingdom First: Starting Churches that Shape Movements, and Kingdom Matrix: Designing Churches for the Kingdom of God.

Developing A Christ Centered Church is a powerful reminder for every church, pastor, and leader that God wants His church to be alive and well. The problem is that we know the problem, but it seems everyone wants to fix it with a program. Programs won't fix the problems of the church. Only Christ as the head of the church can fix His body.

For all of us who have been blessed by previous books by Henry and Richard Blackaby, this book provides sound biblical principles, a Christ-centered focus, and examples of what a healthy New Testament church should look like.

I'm blessed by the personal examples from Henry's life and ministry. We need to listen to those who have gone before us. As I read these pages, I felt like I was on the journey with Henry and his family. In every city in North America, churches are declining or dying. Once vital witnesses, they now stand as symbols of failure – failure that should never happen to a Christ-focused church. This is a book of hope and a challenge to the declining church. These pages are filled with truths that need to be heeded.

> – MICHAEL CATT, Senior Pastor, Sherwood Church, Albany, GA.; Executive Producer, Sherwood Pictures

With approximately 70% of churches plateaued or in decline, the revitalization of the church has become an essential focus. Henry and Richard Blackaby call upon churches to exercise faith, to live in the counsel of God's Word, and to reach beyond what they can do for themselves to trust God for the extraordinary. This volume is based upon Scripture and is filled with wonderful personal stories of God at work to revitalize His church.

> – J. ROBERT WHITE, Executive Director, Georgia Baptist Convention

BLACKABY
MINISTRIES INTERNATIONAL

DEVELOPING A CHRIST-CENTERED CHURCH

PUBLISHED BY BLACKABY MINISTRIES INTERNATIONAL

P.O. Box 1035
Jonesboro, GA 30237
www.blackaby.org

Originally published as: Flickering Lamps: Christ and His Church

ISBN 979-8-9990253-0-2

Publisher's Cataloging-in-Publication data

Names: Blackaby, Henry T., 1935-, author. | Blackaby, Richard, 1961-, author.
Title: Developing a Christ-centered church / Henry & Richard Blackaby.
Description: Jonesboro, GA: Blackaby Ministries International, 2025.
Identifiers: LCCN: 2025910777 | ISBN: 979-8-9990253-0-2
Subjects: LCSH Church growth. | Christian leadership. | Leadership. | Pastoral theology. | Church renewal. | Missions. | Christian life. | BISAC RELIGION / Christian Church / Growth | RELIGION / Christian Living / Leadership & Mentoring
Classification: LCC BV652.1 .B53 2025 | DDC 253--dc23

Printed in the United States of America
2025 — 1st ed

Contents

FORWARD

Across North America today, there are coffee shops, flea markets, condominiums, and even mosques that were once church buildings. More than 4,000 churches in America close their doors each year. Southern Baptists see more than 900 churches disband annually. You might assume the majority of those are located in rural areas where the population is declining, but you would be wrong. More than 75% are in cities with growing populations.

As a church planter for more than 25 years, I ignored the crisis of dying churches. I was convinced that the only way to evangelize North America was to plant new churches. Southern Baptists start more than 1,200 churches every year. Yet, when 900 close annually, there is only a net gain of 300 to 400, which does not even keep up with population growth. North America's lostness compels us to plant new churches and revitalize/re-plant dying ones.

There is also a theological imperative we must address. Scripture is abundantly clear—all things were created to glorify God. The local church engages in ministry, missions, and evangelism to make the gospel known, that people might become followers of Jesus and glorify God with their lives. The local church exists to magnify God. We must, therefore, ask this question: Is there anything about a dying church that brings glory to God? What is there about a dying church that proclaims that God is great and the gospel is powerful? For the glory of God, we must do everything possible to achieve the revitalization and re-planting of dying churches.

The reasons churches die are varied, and the steps necessary to revitalize and re-plant churches are numerous. But one thing is abundantly clear: No change is possible without the repentance of God's people.

Henry and Richard Blackaby are uniquely qualified to teach churches how to seek God's face and hear His voice. No one in my generation has done that better. Speaking from a wellspring of experience and solid biblical insight, the Blackabys have created an invaluable resource.

As I work with Southern Baptists across North America who are seeking to revitalize and re-plant their churches, I enthusiastically recommend this book as the place to begin the process. It is a must-read for every church that is experiencing decline. It not only describes the tenuous situation of a church that is struggling but it also offers real, tangible hope for turning the situation around. Rich in biblical insight, this book offers hope that is not based on human endeavor but on the effectual work of Christ. He has a plan, a purpose, and a promise for every church.

John Mark Clifton
National Legacy Strategy Leader
North American Mission Board of the SBC

PREFACE

Richard and I (Henry) have enjoyed writing numerous books together, and we have been deeply gratified by how God has used them to encourage so many people. Yet this one may be our most important. The existence of thousands of churches is at stake. Today's church is under siege. The media mocks it. Government restricts it. Satan attacks it. Sin permeates it. As a result, hundreds of churches disband every year. Congregations that began with great promise dwindle in numbers, lose hope, and close their doors. That is why we wrote this book.

We were immensely encouraged when John Mark Clifton told us about the initiative he and his team are leading to prevent as many churches as possible from closing. He described how God used our previous writing to preserve pastors who were ready to quit and to reinvigorate churches. He asked us to write something specifically for struggling or declining churches. That project immediately became our top priority. We love the local church. We also delight in watching God demonstrate His power in and through local bodies of believers. We both thoroughly enjoyed being pastors, and we continue to encourage ministers and churches whenever possible.

There is no reason for a church to die, not when Christ is its Head. There are times when churches must make changes, sometimes dramatic ones, but they need not die. God has a purpose for each one. We pray that as you read this material, God will give you a fresh vision of what He intends to do through your church.

Richard played a major role in writing this book, but we felt led to write it using my voice throughout. It traces my journey as the pastor of Faith Baptist Church in Saskatoon, Saskatchewan, Canada. When I arrived, the church was on the brink of disbanding. This book describes the miracles God did not only to revive the church but to multiply its ministry across a nation. I believe God can transform any church if His people surrender themselves fully to Him.

Special thanks to Lisa Blackaby and Carrie Blackaby Camp who diligently edited these pages. Thanks also to Rick Fisher, Sarah Blackaby, Steve Parsons, Jim Redford, and John Mark Clifton for your input and contributions.

We pray that in the years to come, we will hear numerous testimonies from people around the world about the mighty work God did in their church as they trusted Him for a miracle. We know it is possible for a waning church to be reborn into a dynamic band of believers who dispel the darkness in their community and greatly advance God's kingdom. We have experienced that first hand. We pray you will too.

Henry and Richard Blackaby

INTRODUCTION

A CHURCH ABOUT TO DIE

One day I received a phone call that changed my life. In fact, it changed millions of lives. At the time, I was the pastor of a church in Downey, California. Before I arrived as pastor, the church had suffered greatly. Bitter disunity among the members had led to a three-way split. I was called to lead the remnant. During the next five years, the church experienced healing and restoration of its members, a renewed vibrancy in its worship, and an increased ministry to the community. The congregation was spiritually healthy once again, and I loved the church dearly.

Before I was called to the church in Downey, I served as the pastor of a struggling church in San Pablo, which is in the San Francisco Bay Area . It was my first pastorate. The church was located in a crime-riddled, broken community. I performed scores of funerals. Yet I also saw God change numerous lives and heal broken marriages. The local police even credited our church with contributing to a drop in the area's crime rate. Having served fewer than ten years as a pastor, I had already witnessed God's gracious hand working mightily in two unique local churches. But this phone call would take my walk with God, as well as my church experience, to entirely new biblical proportions.

During that phone conversation, I learned of Faith Baptist Church. It was dying. The ten remaining members had placed a "For Sale" sign on the property and were grimly preparing to disband. They needed a miracle to survive, let alone thrive. Sadly, miracles seemed in short supply over the church's turbulent history.

It was located more than 1,700 miles away from Downey, in the agricultural community of Saskatoon, Saskatchewan, Canada. Its population of 120,000 seemed miniscule compared to the teeming masses in the metro Los Angeles area where I then lived. The winters in Saskatoon were brutal, with temperatures dipping lower than forty degrees below zero.

The church had begun in the 1920s as an outreach of a women's mission society. Occasional successes marked its history. Yet every time the church took a step forward, it invariably experienced conflict and weak leadership. After years of disappointment and decline, the church had lost any sense of its original missionary zeal.

Several factors conspired to condemn the small congregation to obscurity. The church was buried deep within a residential neighborhood, making it difficult for even the best-intentioned visitor to find. There was almost no parking space. The building was in pitiful disrepair. The roof hanging over the front entrance sagged so severely that the front door could only be fully opened if people heaved themselves enthusiastically against it. The box-shaped structure was walled in stucco and painted a dreary off-white. Every spring, water from melting snow would seep into the basement, invading the Sunday school rooms and leaving stains and mold wherever it crept. The antiquated tile floor in the auditorium coupled with cheap metal chairs for the congregation contributed to a noisy, less-than-worshipful experience. The meager offerings were insufficient to cover even general maintenance of the aging facility, let alone sorely needed renovations.

Ultimately, the congregation had dwindled to fewer than a dozen members. Because the church could not offer even a token salary, it had been unable to enlist a pastor. With resources exhausted and the people disheartened, disbandment seemed the only remaining option. It appeared that this little congregation would soon become the next in a succession of churches across North America to close its doors permanently.

Then God brought the church to my attention. My wife, Marilynn, and I agreed to pray. As we did, God convinced us that He wanted to restore that church. I decided to visit Saskatoon. God began to reveal His perspective to me. Here was a determined little group of people who tenaciously believed that God still had a purpose for them. God showed me an extensive province, almost the size of Texas, with town after town lacking a gospel witness. He reminded me that churches in Canada were declining. When God revealed to me what was on His heart, it took my breath away.

Leaving California for Saskatoon made no sense. I had four sons under nine years old, with a daughter still to come. I had to think about their future. I also served in the second-largest city in North America. Clearly, that was a strategic place to invest my life. The church I served had experienced many difficulties, but it had regained its health, and I was blessed with many strong, supportive congregational leaders. Members had recently voted to give me a raise, a healthy book allowance, a trip to Israel, and time to work on a doctor's degree. God was using me where I was. Conversely, the future of the church in Saskatchewan seemed much in doubt. Friends and fellow pastors insisted I would be wasting my life and condemning my ministry to irrelevance if I left my thriving California congregation and migrated to a small, isolated community on the Canadian prairie. But God did not view the situation that way.

Prayer can be unsettling, because God uses our conversations with Him to change us. As Marilynn and I prayed, God laid His heart over ours. Somehow, through the divinely mysterious workings of prayer, we grasped the breathtaking love God had for a tiny, impoverished congregation. Christ died for that church. We knew we must go. Moving to Saskatoon was not an expression of our missionary heart or heroism. It was our response to a God who absolutely refused to allow a little congregation to die.

What follows in this book is an account of what God did. Anyone who was there knows it was God. And anyone who shared in our experience believes God could do it again. Your church may be experiencing great difficulty or considering closing. If so, please read these pages carefully, with your spiritual senses open to what God may say to you. I pray He will lay His heart over yours and grant you a spectacular view of what He intends for your church.

◥ CHAPTER ONE

Christ's Purpose for His Church

CHRIST AMONG HIS CHURCHES

No living person had seen what John witnessed. He had been a young man when he encountered Jesus many years earlier. While John was mending fishing nets with his brother James, Jesus passed by their boat and invited them to follow Him (Mark 1:19-20). The next three years were a whirlwind. John experienced miracles that would become legendary. He learned from the greatest teacher in history. His companions were the future apostles of the church. His closest friend was the Son of God.

Much had happened in John's life since the heady days when he was the Messiah's companion. John had become a beloved apostolic father of the Early Church. He had performed miracles and preached countless sermons. Tradition claims he served for a time at the church in Ephesus. John received word on ten different occasions that one of his fellow disciples had been martyred. Great saints like Stephen, James (the brother of Jesus), and Paul had likewise met cruel deaths in Christ's service.

Now an old man, only John remained of the original apostles. Eventually, the authorities came for him too. Under the Roman emperor Diocletian, pressure was mounting against the church. The aged apostle was exiled to the island of Patmos, sixty miles southwest of Ephesus. There he waited not only to learn of his own fate but also to hear news from his beloved churches.

John was praying on the Lord's day. Undoubtedly, he was interceding for the many Christians he knew personally who were in danger of persecution by the Roman authorities. He may have wondered if the churches would withstand the evil onslaught that loomed before them.

Suddenly, John was startled by a loud voice that pierced the air like a trumpet (Rev. 1:10). When the apostle turned to see who was speaking, this is what he saw:

> *"... when I turned I saw seven golden lampstands, and among the lampstands was One like the Son of Man, dressed in a long robe, and with a gold sash wrapped around His chest. His head and hair were white like wool—white as snow, His eyes like a fiery flame, His feet like fine bronze fired in a furnace, and His voice like the sound of cascading waters. In His right hand He had seven stars; from His mouth came a sharp two-edged sword; and His face was shining like the sun at midday" (Rev. 1:12-16).*

John was so overwhelmed at the sight of the risen Christ that he fell to the ground as if he were dead (Rev. 1:17). Though John had spent more than three years in Jesus' company and served Him for many decades, the awesome sight of the exalted Christ terrified the veteran apostle. In response, the Lord laid His right hand upon His faithful servant and declared,

> *"Don't be afraid! I am the First and the Last, and the Living One, I was dead, but look—I am alive forever and ever, and I hold the keys of death and Hades... The secret of the seven stars you saw in My right hand, and the seven golden lampstands, is this: the seven stars are the angels of the seven churches, and the seven lampstands are the seven churches" (Rev. 1:17-20).*

The exalted Christ had an inspiring message for the elderly disciple and the churches under his care. Christ walked among the seven lampstands. The lampstands represented the seven churches of Asia. The Son of Man held the angels of the churches in His immensely powerful right hand. I believe the angels of the churches were their pastors. How comforting to know that the Alpha and Omega, the One who owns the keys to death and Hades, holds pastors firmly in His grip! Though the church's enemies might try their hardest, Christ stood triumphantly among His churches. No words could be more comforting to a persecuted church than that Christ, the victor over every enemy of humanity, stood among them and held their pastors in His hand.

MISSING ITS PURPOSE

The risen Christ gave John a message for the seven churches scattered throughout the Roman province of Asia. For each church, Christ pointed out practices He commended. In five cases, He also identified behaviors He found intolerable. The first congregation Christ addressed was in Ephesus.

"To the angel of the church in Ephesus write: 'The one who holds the seven stars in His right hand and who walks among the seven gold lampstands says: I know your works, your labor, and your endurance, and that you cannot tolerate evil. You have tested those who call themselves apostles and are not, and you have found them to be liars. You also possess endurance and have tolerated many things because of My name, and have not grown weary. But I have this against you: you have abandoned the love you had at first. Remember then how far you have fallen; repent, and do the works you did at first. Otherwise, I will come to you and remove your lampstand from its place—unless you repent.

'Yet you do have this: you hate the practices of the Nicolai-
tans, which I also hate. Anyone who has an ear should listen
to what the Spirit says to the churches. I will give the victor
the right to eat from the tree of life, which is in the paradise
of God'" (Rev 2:1-7).

Perhaps only the church in Jerusalem had received as much
from God as the church at Ephesus had. The apostle Paul established it (Acts 18:19-21). Paul spent three years teaching and
preaching in Ephesus (Acts 19). He later claimed of his time with
them, *"for three years I did not cease to warn everyone night and day*
with tears" (Acts 20:31). God worked powerfully through Paul's
ministry, performing numerous miracles and casting out many
demons (Acts 19:11-12). Many other church luminaries ministered
in Ephesus. Apollos, the famed orator, preached in the city (Acts
18:24- 28). Priscilla and Aquila ministered there, as did Silas, Luke,
Tychicus, Timothy, and John (Acts 15:40; 18:18- 19; Eph. 6:21; 1 Tim.
1:3). Jesus cautioned, *"Much will be required of everyone who has*
been given much. And even more will be expected of the one who has
been entrusted with more" (Luke 12:48). When churches are given
much, God expects much from them in return. God obviously had
a special purpose for the Ephesians, since He generously provided
them with many of the finest leaders and teachers in the world.

Ephesus was a major city in the Roman Empire, a prosperous
seaport and a hub for international trade. It boasted one of the
seven wonders of the ancient world, the temple to Diana (Acts 19:21-
41). This major center of pagan idolatry dominated local commerce
and demanded the loyalty of its citizens. The city also housed
the temple to Emperor Diocletian, motivating the Ephesians to
prove their loyalty to the Roman emperor and his designs, even if
it meant persecuting the church. From Ephesus, one could easily
travel around the province of Asia. While Paul was in Ephesus, the

church may have sent out church planters throughout the region. Clearly, it was a strategic location for spreading the gospel.

With such a solid spiritual foundation, the Christians at Ephesus did many things well. They tested those who called themselves apostles and exposed the charlatans (Rev. 2:2). They also despised the heretical teachings of the Nicolaitans. Having been instructed by teachers such as Paul, Timothy, and John, their doctrine remained orthodox. They also refused to tolerate evil (Rev. 2:2). The church continued to labor, persevere, and endure trials, such as the apostle John's arrest. For the most part, the church's behavior was admirable.

The Ephesian church must have been gratified to hear Christ commend them for so many behaviors and then devastated when He declared, *"But I have this against you"* (Rev. 2:5). How sublime it is when Christ has no caveats in His evaluation of a church or individual! Yet it takes just one sin to make us deserving of judgment.

Christ had called the Ephesian church into a personal, loving relationship with Himself. Nothing could be more significant. They had a solid list of exceptional behavior and only one shortcoming: "... *you have abandoned the love you had at first*" (Rev. 2:4). That lone sin negated everything that was praiseworthy, for they had neglected what was most critical. In their zeal to be doctrinally, morally, and methodologically orthodox, their hearts had shifted from their Savior. They were still working for Christ, but they were no longer devoted to Him. They had overlooked the most important mandate: love the Lord God with all their heart, soul, mind, and strength (Mark 12:30).

Christ's response to the church's waning love was decisive: *"Remember then how far you have fallen; repent, and do the works you did at first. Otherwise, I will come to you and remove your lampstand*

from its place—unless you repent" (Rev. 2:5). Christ's declaration
might appear harsh. After all, the church's conduct was generally
admirable. But Christ will not tolerate a church that forgets its
purpose. A church that forfeits its highest calling is in danger
of losing its way and suffering God's judgment. The church at
Ephesus had no time to lose. It needed to return wholeheartedly
to its Lord. Despite its fidelity to proper doctrine, the Ephesian
church was unacceptable to God. Clearly, even the most influential
churches in the world can lose their way.

THE THREE PURPOSES OF THE CHURCH

God created the church for His eternal purposes. Christ is
its Head (Col. 1:18), and He is the One who builds it (Matt. 16:18). I
believe Scripture teaches that God has three primary purposes
for the church: to glorify God, to make disciples, and to bless its
community. When local congregations fulfill these purposes,
they have God's power, pleasure, and provision at their disposal.
When churches forsake God's purposes, they invite His judgment
(Rev. 2:5).

1. To Glorify God

The apostle Paul declared, *"Now to Him who is able to do above
and beyond all that we ask or think— according to the power that works
in you—to Him be glory in the church and in Christ Jesus to all gen-
erations..."* (Eph. 3:20-21). Paul also said of Christ, *"For from Him
and through Him and to Him are all things. To Him be glory forever"*
(Rom. 11:36). The ultimate purpose of every Christian is to glorify
God. There is no higher calling. Some churches focus on what they
believe. Sound doctrine is important. But as Scripture teaches, faith
and doctrine apart from God-glorifying action are dead (James

2:17-19). Other congregations assume that doing good deeds brings God glory. But the Bible teaches that God's ways are not our ways (Is. 55:8-9). It is possible to do a good deed and yet dishonor God in the process. The key to glorifying God is to love Him and serve Him *His way*. Every church must ask this pivotal question: Are we bringing glory to God by our actions? If not, repentance is in order. Any church that is not exalting Christ by its behavior has lost its reason to exist.

2. To Make Disciples

A second purpose of the church is to make disciples throughout the world. Jesus' final command was, *"Go, therefore, and make disciples of all nations, baptizing them in the name of the Father and of the Son and of the Holy Spirit, teaching them to observe everything I have commanded you"* (Matt. 28:18-20). Disciples do not just *believe* in Christ; they *follow* Him. Churches are called to reach out worldwide, not just to the people in their zip code. God designed churches to be world mission strategy centers. With Christ as its Head, one local church can extend God's kingdom around the world. Churches that are failing to fulfill this mandate are falling short of God's purpose.

3. To Preserve and Bless Their Communities

Jesus commanded His disciples to be salt and light wherever they went (Matt. 5:13-16). In Jesus' day, without refrigeration, meat and other foods would quickly spoil. Salt prevented valuable food items from rotting. Likewise, Jesus said Christians are to act as a preserving agent for their communities. Sin naturally tears down marriages, families, economies, and societies, but righteousness protects people from the ravages of evil.

Scripture likens evil in the world to darkness (Luke 22:53). Jesus entered the world as light to cast out darkness from the earth (John 1:4-5). Evil constantly strives to snuff out the light and leave the world in shadows. Yet wherever a light shines brightly, darkness disappears. Jesus told believers to *"Let your light shine before men that they may see your good works and glorify My Father in heaven"* (Matt. 5:16). The book of Revelation portrays churches as golden lampstands (Rev. 1:20). While John was on the Isle of Patmos, some of the lamps were beginning to flicker, and the risen Christ sent a message to beware, lest darkness overtake them.

God expects Christians to make a positive difference in the world. When God sent word to the Israelites, who had been exiled to Babylon, He urged them to *"Seek the welfare of the city I have deported you to. Pray to the Lord on its behalf, for when it has prosperity, you will prosper"* (Jer. 29:7). God commanded His people to bless their community, even when they were living in enemy territory! The writer of Proverbs declared, *"When the righteous thrive, a city rejoices"* (Prov. 11:10). God's people are to be both a preservative and a blessing wherever He plants them.

As a pastor, I took this exhortation seriously. I expected our church to exert a positive influence on our community and to dispel darkness from it. Jesus declared, *"... on this rock I will build My church, and the forces of Hades will not overpower it"* (Matt. 16:18). I trusted God to use our church to bring the gates of hell down in our neighborhood. We saw God restore marriages, encourage prodigal children to return, set alcoholics free, reform criminals, make public schools more wholesome, close local businesses promoting immorality, and help ministries to the poor and needy flourish.

There are churches that could shut down today and their community would never know they were gone. Nothing in the neighborhood or city would change. How tragic! God intends for local churches to be such a blessing to their community that even unbelievers would be saddened if they closed their doors.

A SPECIFIC PURPOSE

God has three overriding purposes for every church, regardless of its location or demographics: glorify God, make disciples, and bless the community.

In addition to these general purposes, God gives local churches specific assignments or a focus that drives much of what they do. The church at Antioch was assigned to extend the gospel to the Gentiles (Acts 13:1-3). The church at Jerusalem demonstrated a special concern for widows and the city's poor (Acts 4:34-37; 6:1-7). The church at Ephesus was strong in doctrine and exposing false teaching (Rev. 2:2). The church at Philippi felt compelled to invest financially in missionary work (Phil. 4:14-18).

Some churches are located near a universities and focus on reaching students and faculty. Other congregations are established in the inner city to minister to addicts, prostitutes, and the homeless. A church may be planted in a section of the city where there is a dense collection of a particular immigrant population. Churches have been founded specifically to reach bikers, cowboys, truckers, soldiers, or businesspeople. Some older churches become incubators for new church plants. Of course, churches must reach all types of people, but sometimes God gives a church a particular assignment that lends a unique focus to its ministry.

Members of a new church usually have a keen understanding of their focus. Over time, that sense of purpose may fade. Rather than being on mission with God, churches can degenerate into religious bureaucracies that are more concerned with filling vacancies on their committees than with impacting their community.

Perhaps a church is located across the street from a university, but no students or faculty attend. Maybe it meets in a subdivision, but none of its members live in the neighborhood.

At times, churches become so fixated on maintaining their facility that they forget why God commissioned them in the first place. It is helpful to remember that in more than two thousand years of church history, God has never established a church for the purpose of property upkeep! Church buildings are simply a means to an end. When churches obsess over secondary matters, they have lost sight of their God-given mission. According to Revelation 2:5, that is a precarious place for a church to be.

A CHURCH THAT FORGOT ITS PURPOSE

I will never forget driving up to Faith Baptist Church in Saskatoon for the first time. It was evident that the church was not fulfilling its divine purpose. The building's appearance reflected its tired, demoralized occupants. The tiny congregation fretted about paying bills but spoke little about reaching the community. They debated their past but voiced no plans for the future. Without a compelling mission, the embattled members were merely trying to survive.

GLORIFYING GOD

No one who drove by our building was struck by God's greatness. The "For Sale" sign cried out "FAILURE," not "VICTORY." The dirty, unkempt appearance of the church building did not inspire anyone to ponder God's grandeur. The conflict-filled business meetings demonstrated no evidence that the Lord of the universe was the Head of that church.

I often see churches take pride in paying their bills on time, maintaining their grounds, or preserving the carpets from wear and tear. While it is true that we must be good stewards of whatever God places in our hands, let me be clear: choirs of angels do not burst into praise when they look down from heaven and see that the hallways in the Sunday school area are free from scuff marks! Balancing the books, mowing lawns, and mopping floors are not the primary ways churches glorify their Savior. After all, cults and stores selling pornography do those things. Churches glorify God when they focus on what He cares about—when they act, talk, and look like Christ.

The dispirited church in Canada was not accurately representing their holy, all-powerful God. The only ministries the people undertook were those they thought they could afford, which was not much. They argued often. I learned that one of the few remaining members had left the church when I was called as pastor because he believed they should have chosen to disband instead. The church was not seeking what was on God's heart. Instead, they concentrated on electric bills, water drainage issues, and aging copier machines. As the new pastor, I realized we had to repent of losing our first love and return to the Head of our church.

MAKING DISCIPLES

The small remnant in Saskatoon consisted of mostly middle-aged and older adults. There were no children or youth. It was an aging, dying congregation. When I first toured the facility, I passed some vacant Sunday school rooms. Those spaces once held children who were studying the Bible; some classrooms still had pictures and art projects exhibited on the walls from former students. Sadly, the educational space had become a museum to the past rather than a training ground for the future.

The church was founded by a women's missionary society. They had envisioned reaching a new neighborhood in the city. That evangelistic vision had dissipated. Not only had the church never started a mission church but it had failed to reach its own community. The baptistry sat unused. The members had never taken a mission trip or sent out a missionary. The congregation had failed to make disciples as Jesus commanded, and now it was at death's door.

PRESERVING AND BLESSING ITS COMMUNITY

I had no doubt that those few remaining members had tried to be faithful. They continued to hold services. They valiantly attempted to keep the building serviceable. Yet they had not reached their community. A modest sign informing passers-by of the service times was posted on the side of the building. But had you entered, you would have found fewer than a dozen people huddled together for worship. Most of the remaining members did not even live in the neighborhood.

It struck me that if the church disbanded and the property were transformed into a community hall offering Tuesday Night Bingo, many in the neighborhood would be delighted. The stark truth was that this little church made absolutely no difference to the community. It did not even pay taxes, so some viewed it as a financial drain. If our church had closed, it is doubtful that people in the area would have noticed any difference. The surrounding residents felt no connection to a little congregation that had made no effort to impact the community.

A SPECIAL PURPOSE

I always find churches' names interesting. Ironically, when a church endures a nasty split, the splinter group often adopts a name such as "Unity" or "Harmony." Some of the least friendly churches in the city have been named "Friendship." When the founders of this particular church considered names, they chose "Faith." I never knew the founders, but I suspect they envisioned a church that would house people of robust and vibrant faith. In later years, the church indeed lived up to its name.

I can only imagine what passers-by must have thought as they drove past "Faith" Baptish Church and observed the "For Sale" sign out front. The church had diligently tried to live within its means, never attempting anything that required God's miraculous provision. It was abundantly clear that when the church initiated only what it could afford, it made no impression on its community (Acts 2:40-47). The church had been launched with a self-proclaimed calling to be a people of faith, but it had forsaken that special purpose along the way.

REPENT!

When the risen Christ walked among the lampstands in John's day, His eyes were like a flame, and His face shone as brightly as the sun at midday (Rev. 1:14-16). His holy inspection cut through all pretense and masquerades. Deception melted before His scrutiny. He saw everything clearly. When He cast His gaze upon the church at Ephesus, He found a congregation that had lost its first love. They were still busy with religious activities, but their hearts had shifted away from Him.

Fortunately, the fiery eyes of the risen Christ saw more than the church's shortcomings; they also saw the cure. The Lord instructed the church to do three things. First, they were to remember how far they had fallen. God's people often have no concept of how far they have drifted from God.

Second, they were to *repent*. The church at Ephesus might have assumed they had no problem with their hearts, just their calendars. God viewed the situation differently. Busyness that distracts from God is sin, and the only remedy is repentance. The congregation at Ephesus did not need to rearrange their schedule; they needed to adjust their hearts.

Finally, they were to *"do the works you did at first"* (Rev. 2:5). The Ephesians needed to serve God out of love and devotion. A change in action would indicate a change in heart.

◢ CHALLENGE

Hundreds of thousands of churches claiming millions of members are scattered across America today. Yet the nation is suffering moral, spiritual, and ethical decay. People are leaving the church in droves. The media makes a public mockery of Christian beliefs. Society is steadily pushing the church to the periphery; it is no longer being taken seriously. Thousands of churches are closing, and hundreds of pastors are leaving the ministry each year. There is no time for excuses or delays.

The risen Christ walks among today's churches. His fiery eyes see past your activities, programs, and doctrines, straight to your heart. Are you as devoted to Him as you once were? Have you remained focused on your divine purpose? Is your church clearly enjoying God's blessing? Is God working powerfully in your midst? Is the community around your church being changed for the better by your presence? Heed the words of the risen Christ: *"Remember then how far you have fallen; repent, and do the works you did at first. Otherwise, I will come to you and remove your lampstand from its place—unless you repent."*

◢ QUESTIONS FOR REFLECTION

1. What did the founders have in mind when they started your church? Were they striving to reach a specific people group? Was the church intended to have a unique quality or focus?

2. How has your church changed since it was established? Are those changes positive?

3. How does your church glorify God? What are some ways your church is not glorifying God as it should?

4. In what ways is your church making or failing to make disciples? Are you focused on making disciples "of all nations"? How?

5. How is your church's presence currently having a positive impact on your community? What are some ways your church could be a visible and practical blessing on the neighborhood? Would people miss your church if it closed?

6. Does your church need to repent of some sins?

◥ CHAPTER TWO

Christ's Plans for His Church

Moses knew God's purpose for the Israelites—freedom from bondage in Egypt. But Moses was mistaken when he assumed he knew God's *plans*. He murdered an Egyptian taskmaster who was abusing a Hebrew (Ex. 2:11-15). Using the wrong plan to accomplish the right purpose cost Moses forty years in the wilderness. Unfortunately, Moses never fully learned that lesson. When God told Moses to provide water for the Israelites from a rock, God also shared the plan: speak to the rock. Moses opted for his own method: striking it. That seemingly innocuous presumption cost Moses the opportunity to join the Israelites in the Promised Land (Num. 20:1-13).

Gideon understood God's purpose to free the Israelites from the oppression of the Midianites. He assumed the plan was to muster as many Israelite soldiers as possible. He extended a call, and 32,000 soldiers responded (Judg. 6:34-7:3). But that was not God's plan, despite how reasonable it may have seemed to Gideon. So God had Gideon reduce his force to a mere 300 men. No general, not even Alexander the Great, would devise a plan to rout more than 100,000 enemy soldiers with a 300-man army. But God did.

I have been privileged to travel around the world and meet many pastors and church leaders from a wide array of denominations. These dear people truly want to glorify God and bless their community. The problems generally arise while constructing a plan.

A church might say, "Jesus commanded us to make disciples of all nations, so let's get to work! Let's plan a mission trip to Cambodia. Perhaps we should also start a Bible study for local businesspeople each Wednesday at noon. And we can't forget the children—let's begin a Wednesday evening children's program. And shouldn't we also have day camps in the summer?"

Of course, those activities are good. But the church was commissioned to do *God* things, not *good* things. We do not think the way God does. He declared, *"'For My thoughts are not your thoughts, and your ways are not My ways.' This is the Lord's declaration. 'For as heaven is higher than earth, so My ways are higher than your ways, and My thoughts than your thoughts'"* (Is. 55:8-9). It is arrogant to assume that God leaves it up to the local church to determine how to glorify Him and carry out the Great Commission.

Jesus said, *"... I will build My church... "* (Matt. 16:18). Scripture also states, *"But now God has placed the parts, each one of them, in the body just as He wanted"* (1 Cor. 12:18). Christ not only builds His church but He also directs it. When Christ said He was the Head of the Church, He was not referring to His role as a token, nominal figurehead (Col. 1:18). He intends to be actively involved in every aspect of church life. And, as we saw in Revelation 1-3, He will hold churches accountable for how they conduct themselves under His leadership.

I KNOW YOUR WORKS

When John encountered his Savior on the Isle of Patmos, the Head of the Church had a message for the seven churches in Asia: Ephesus, Smyrna, Pergamum, Thyatira, Sardis, Philadelphia, and Laodicea. Some of these congregations were wealthy, while others had little. Several faced persecution. Each congregation was presumably doing what they thought was best. Yet the key to a church's success is not feeling good about its ministry but pleasing the risen Christ.

In John's revelation, Christ spoke a word for each church. He walked among the lampstands. His fiery eyes had examined their works. To each church, Christ declared, *"I know your works"* (Rev. 2:2, 9, 13, 19; 3:1, 8, 15). To Ephesus, Christ declared, *"But I have this against you, you have abandoned the love you had at first"* (Rev. 2:4). To Smyrna, He said, *"But I have a few things against you. You have some there who hold to the teachings of Balaam, who taught Balak to place a stumbling block in front of the sons of Israel: to eat meat sacrificed to idols and to commit sexual immorality. In the same way, you also have those who hold to the teaching of the Nicolaitans"* (Rev. 2:14-15). To Sardis, Christ declared, *"For I have not found your works complete before My God"* (Rev. 3:2). To Laodicea, Christ announced, *"I know your works, that you are neither cold nor hot. I wish that you were cold or hot. So, because you are lukewarm, and neither hot nor cold, I am going to vomit you out of My mouth"* (Rev. 3:15-16).

Surely, none of these churches intended to displease their Lord. Their leaders probably believed in the efficacy of their methods. But God was not pleased. The Ephesian Christians did many things well, but their hearts had been distracted from their Lord. Perhaps the church at Smyrna was trying to "show grace" and be "inclusive," but Christ was against their strategy.

To Sardis, Christ said their works were incomplete. Maybe the believers at Sardis did only what they could afford rather than what God instructed. They might have been surprised to learn that Christ expected far more from them. To the church at Laodicea, Christ said He knew their works. In their case, the problem was not so much their actions but their attitude. They may have meant well, but they failed to realize that it was not just *what* they did that mattered but *how* they did it. The Laodicean church was serving Christ in a lukewarm, prideful, lackadaisical manner. They had no idea Christ was preparing to spew them out of His mouth.

Many churches across our land need a word from the risen Christ. Their programming is full, their calendars are brimming, and their numbers are slightly ahead of last year. All seems well. Yet Christ would declare to them, "But I have this against you. I know your works!" The church leaders in Ephesus and Laodicea may have been shocked by Christ's message. They assumed He was pleased with them and their activities. But Christ does not measure success the same way the world does. Beautiful buildings, burgeoning attendance, and well-planned services are an abomination to Christ when they are achieved in a manner that dishonors Him. The church at Ephesus boasted one of the most illustrious pedigrees in church history. Yet, unbeknownst to them, the risen Christ was preparing to remove their lampstand if they did not repent.

TRUSTING GOD FOR OUR PLANS

When I arrived at the church in Saskatoon, I was taken aback by how many things desperately needed attention. The building required repainting and refurbishing inside and out. Weeping tile was necessary to prevent the basement from flooding. Hurting members needed care. Where to begin? I had been the pastor of two other congregations, so I was familiar with church programming and administrative issues. I had started successful ministries in my previous churches. I contemplated whether I should implement some of those same programs in my new church. But to be honest, as I pulled up in front of the church after my 1,700-mile odyssey from California, my heart was heavy. "Lord," I prayed. "Where do I start?"

I have learned that developing my own plans and then asking God to bless them does not honor Him. God already has a plan. Noah did not develop a strategy and then pray for God to bless it. He had never heard of an ark before! I needed to cry out to God and beseech Him to reveal His plans to me. My church already had the Holy Spirit present within it (1 Cor. 2:9-12). He would guide us into the will of the Father.

I also learned that if I prayed for God to guide me, I had better keep my spiritual eyes open. It did not take long for God to begin revealing His plans for our church. The same afternoon we arrived in Saskatoon, a car containing five men pulled up in front of our house. The men had driven from Prince Albert, which was 90 miles away. They had been praying earnestly about starting a church in their city, and they had come to ask if I would be their pastor too. We had not even unpacked our suitcases, and God had already revealed where we were to begin our first mission!

Logically, sponsoring a mission church in Prince Albert was absurd. In the month before I arrived in Saskatoon, the church's offerings totaled $90. I had just arrived with my family of six (to be seven by the year's end). I had also brought a worship minister and his family of five. A church of ten people had just called two full-time staff people who had wives and eight children between them. Surely that was a big enough stretch for the first year! I had never heard of a church starting a mission on the day its pastor arrived. Conventional wisdom suggested our priority should be to strengthen the mother church first. Once the home base was strong and had a deeper financial foundation we would be in a position to plant other churches. Yet God declared from the outset that His plan for growing our church would be for us to give ourselves away.

We could not have known that the hallmark of our church over the next decade would be missions. During the twelve years I served as pastor, our church and its missions planted 38 churches and missions. We could never have conceived of that approach on our own. But it was God's plan.

As we continued seeking God's guidance for our church, we sensed He was giving us a second assignment: ministering to the largest institution in the city, the University of Saskatchewan. We believed one of the purposes God originally had for our church when He placed us near the university was to reach future leaders of Canada for Christ. Once again, this plan presented several logistical challenges. The first was the target group. We were a small church with pitifully few resources. Everyone knows university students have no money. Even if we managed to reach them, they would be unable to contribute significant finances to our church.

A second problem was that college students eventually graduate. It could seem like wasted effort to concentrate on reaching a population that would eventually relocate to start their careers. Common sense suggested we devote our attention to reaching white-collar adults so we could develop a financial base before we focused on missions and college students.

Third, despite having been the pastor of two churches, I had no history with college students. It seemed logical for me to begin ministering in areas of my strengths and experience. If we had developed our own agenda for our church, that may well have been what we did. But we were not trying to make our own plans. We did not want to give an account to the Head of our church and have Him pronounce, "But I have this against you!"

Another pragmatic consideration we faced in beginning a college ministry was that not a single student or faculty member attended our church. We could have brainstormed how to gain a foothold on the campus or launched a marketing campaign to attract students' attention. But we had no money. If we based our ministry to students on what we could afford, we would have planned to do nothing. Instead, we asked God to show us how to reach university students for Christ.

Can you guess who the first person I baptized was? A professor of law at the university! He was soon playing a key role in our little church. We connected the spiritual dots and recognized that God was working out His plans for our congregation.

One day I received a call at my office from a minister to college students in Seattle, Washington. She wanted to bring a team of students to our city that summer and wondered if we could use her help in starting a ministry to the university. By the end of that summer, we had a core group of students, and one of the mission team members had decided to serve with us for two more years. Step by step, God unfolded His plan. Whenever we did not know what to do next, we waited on the Lord until He showed us.

As we continued ministering at the university, we believed we should try to reach out to the students in the dorms. The problem was that none of the students who attended our church lived on campus. One day, I gathered a small group of students together. I had been impressed by the words Jesus—the sinless, perfect Son of God—used to explain His approach to ministry: *"I assure you: The Son is not able to do anything on His own, but only what He sees the Father doing. For whatever the Father does, the Son also does these things in the same way. For the Father loves the Son and shows Him everything He is doing..."* (John 5:19-20). I told that group of young people that God commissioned us to reach the university, and He would show us how to make inroads into the student dorms. The key was learning to recognize where He was already working and then to join Him.

The next week, one of those students was surprised when a classmate invited her for coffee. She hardly knew the classmate, but she had committed to keeping her spiritual eyes open. She agreed to go. Over coffee, her new friend asked, "Are you a Christian?" She went on to explain that she lived in the dorm. She and eight other girls were trying to study the Bible, but they did not know how. She asked the young lady from our church to help them. Three Bible studies ultimately developed in the women's dorm and two in the men's. What happened? We realized God would not only tell us *what* to do but He would also show us *how* to do what He asked. Doing things God's way makes all the difference.

God ultimately led us to undertake another major project: establishing a Bible college. Many of the university students we reached felt called to minister in our mission churches, but they had no training. For some, traveling to the United States to attend seminary was not an option. We believed God wanted us to do what Jesus did with His disciples—train them ourselves. I had never even taught a college class, let alone started a school. Nevertheless, it became clear God was leading our church, which was running fewer than 100 people at the time, to start a Bible college. I told some other pastors what God was leading us to do, and they graciously agreed to travel long distances to teach at the school for free. God granted us favor with donors.

Just as God intended, the various ministries He led us to begin dovetailed perfectly. We reached dozens of college students for Christ. Many of those students felt God calling them into pastoral ministry and enrolled in our Bible college. Every Sunday we sent students across the province to preach, lead music, and teach Sunday school at our various missions. I prayed urgently each week, as I knew students were driving snow-covered highways in ancient vehicles held together by prayer and duct tape. Words cannot express how vibrant our church became. Young adults eagerly served in various capacities. During prayer meetings, students would cry out for those who needed Christ. Soon afterward, they would walk the aisle at the close of a service with the person they had prayed for in tow.

We scheduled times for church members to share what God was doing in their lives. So many would speak that I would sometimes not have time to preach my sermon. Those were amazing days. I would look out over an auditorium filled with passionate followers of Christ, many of them new Christians, and remember the ten discouraged people waiting for me when I first arrived. Not only had God always had a unique purpose for our church but He also had plans to help us achieve it. We simply had to listen to Him and obey.

As our congregation walked with God, He led us in specific ways. He also taught us some fundamental principles we applied to all we did.

1. Seek First the Kingdom of God

Jesus clearly told His people what a church's priority should be: *"But seek first the kingdom of God and His righteousness, and all these things will be provided for you"* (Matt. 6:33). Christ did not command us to build our church; He said *He* would do that (Matt. 16:18). He told us to make His kingdom the focus of our life. There is a big difference between building a church and building God's kingdom.

Selfishness strangles churches. I have seen it happen many times. While we were in the midst of starting several missions across our province, I received word that a large congregation wanted to send us their missions offering for that year. We were thrilled and saw the donation as an answer to prayer. We began calculating how many new churches we could launch with the promised funds. Then I received an anguished call from one of the church's pastors. Apparently, some church members had chafed at the idea of giving such a large donation to missions. They wanted to build a second gymnasium on their own campus instead. And they did. The proposed offering seemed like simply too much money to "give away." I was heartbroken. I knew God could use another means to provide the funds we needed, but I sensed that the church was in danger of slowly suffocating on its self-centeredness. They had become far more focused on building their church than on expanding God's kingdom.

Self-centeredness can creep into churches in many ways. A church may be unwilling to part with its funds, musicians, or volunteers, even though nearby congregations could desperately use them. Perhaps it steadily decreases its contributions to cooperative missions enterprises in order to free up more funds for internal programs. Rather than donating its resources to churches in need, it hoards them in dusty storage rooms.

Few things are less honoring to God than a selfish person or church.

2. Let God Direct Your Steps

Proverbs 3:5-6 counsels, "*Trust in the Lord with all your heart, and do not rely on your own understanding; think about Him in all your ways, and He will guide you on the right paths.*" We came to view this passage not just as an encouraging devotional thought but as highly practical advice. Whether we were undertaking a building program, calling a mission pastor, or operating a Bible college, we needed God to direct our paths.

Do not assume God will merely give you broad principles and then leave you to figure out the details on your own. Our ways are not God's ways! As the prophet Isaiah promised, *"and whenever you turn to the right or to the left, your ears will hear His command behind you: 'This is the way. Walk in it'"* (Is. 30:21). As a church, we learned to trust the divine voice whispering instructions over our shoulder

3. Give Yourself Away

Jesus said, *"For whoever wants to save his life will lose it, but whoever loses his life because of Me will find it"* (Matt. 16:25). One of the most insidious lies Satan whispers into churches' ears is that they should wait to obey God until they have the necessary resources. For years I heard church leaders explain why they could not afford to do what God commanded: *We desperately need a youth minister to care for the teenagers God is sending us, but we cannot afford to hire one right now... God told us to plant a church in a new subdivision opening in our city, but we cannot spare any people or funds... Our church has been invited to assist Christians in a formerly closed country, but the trip might strain our church's budget...* The truth is that you will rarely be able to afford to do what God asks, because He wants you to rely on His provision. The question is not, "Can we afford to obey?" The crucial question is, "Can we afford not to obey?" When we step out in faith, He provides what we lack. I have watched too many churches wait for a more convenient time to obey God, but that time never came.

While I was a pastor in Saskatoon, people often warned me that I would ruin our church if I led my flock to keep giving their time and money to missions. They said I needed to grow my church until it was running at least 500 people each week and then I could start a mission church. I suspect if we had waited until we reached that milestone, we still would not have believed we were ready. Better to obey God immediately. We can become so concerned with what it might cost us to obey that we fail to consider the tragic price of *disobedience*. You are never more like Jesus than when you give yourself away (Phil. 2:5-11).

4. Love One Another

Jesus could not have been any clearer when He said, *"This is My command: love one another as I have loved you"* (John 15:12). Loving our brother is not optional. It is a command. Loving others provides compelling proof that you belong to Christ (1 John 2:9). Part of the reason the church in Saskatoon had declined so drastically was because its members failed to love one another. Bitter arguments ensued over trivial matters. Members refused to forgive each other. People angrily left the church if they did not get their way. The Holy Spirit refused to bless such behavior.

While I was in Saskatoon, I used to pray with a pastor from a sister denomination. Bill McLeod was deeply burdened for his church and prayed fervently for revival. There seemed to be a spiritual logjam quenching the work of the Holy Spirit in his congregation. Two brothers were estranged. They had exchanged unkind words and harbored resentment until their families ultimately stopped socializing with each other. For the previous two years, they had refused to speak to one another. They would sit on opposite sides of the auditorium. When the church scheduled a revival meeting, both brothers attended. One evening before the service began, McLeod met with the siblings in the church basement and challenged their unloving attitudes.

Eventually, the Holy Spirit broke through the impasse. The two men embraced and wept so loudly the people in the auditorium upstairs heard their sobs. That evening they stood before the congregation and confessed their sin. Revival erupted in that church. Many others confessed their own sins. Crowds swelled to the point that the church building could no longer contain everyone. The church rented a larger venue and quickly outgrew it. The meetings continued for seven weeks, with one building after another becoming too small for the growing number of participants. People traveled to Saskatoon from around the world to witness the revival. It spread to other cities across North America and then to other continents. That mighty movement of God became known as The Canadian Revival.

Too often we tolerate unloving attitudes in our midst. At first, only a few people may exhibit ungodly behavior. But over time, unloving attitudes and behaviors can spread like a disease until undercurrents of bitterness permeate a congregation. The fastest way for a church to experience revival is to return to a love relationship with Christ and with one another.

Christ wanted our church to be more than an institution; He wanted it to be a family. Organizations experience ebbs and flows in attendance. Families care for each other, regardless of a person's behavior. A female college student from our congregation went through a difficult time in her life and was enticed to join a cult. She told us she was no longer a part of our church and did not desire any further contact. I told my flock, "We made a covenant with her when she joined our church that regardless of what happened to her, good or bad, we would stand with her. She has been deceived by a lie and she needs us more than ever." When church members reached out to her, she reacted angrily. We continued loving her anyway. When she went through an official membership ceremony at her new "church," some people from Faith Baptist Church attended and prayed for her during the entire service. Eventually, she realized she had been deceived, and she returned to us humbled but grateful we never stopped loving her.

As a pastor, I learned that the way our church loved one member showed everyone else how we would treat them too. If a member fell into sin and the church shunned him, others knew what to expect if they ever became ensnared by sin. If someone left the church and no one pursued her, others knew no one would come searching for them either. I have seen churches that were running 1,000 people on Sundays dwindle to a dozen remaining members. As people left, those who remained criticized the "deserters" and refused to reach out to them. As a result, more and more people left. Cults try to retain members through fear, intimidation, and manipulation. Churches keep their members with love. A church that loses its love will soon lose its people. You cannot prevent people from leaving your fellowship, but you can and should keep loving them. It is much easier to leave an organization than it is to abandon a family.

▲ CONCLUSION

Your best plans will not build God's kingdom. That is God's job. But you can wholly surrender to Christ's lordship and allow Him to build His kingdom through you. If you place your plans, your building, your budget, your programs, and your preferences on the altar, Christ will use your church mightily for His purposes. Have you sought His heart and mind for your church? Are you prepared to do whatever He asks? What God tells you to do may be difficult, even costly. But with His command comes His powerful presence. It is an awesome thing to be on mission with God!

◢ QUESTIONS FOR REFLECTION

1. Has your congregation sought to know God's plans as fervently as it has pursued God's purposes?

2. What is one ministry in your church you could not have developed without God's leading?

3. Are you more focused on building your church or on building God's kingdom?

4. Some churches get the "big picture" from God and then work out the details themselves. Others wait on God to reveal His plan for the details. Which kind of church is yours?

5. Is your church more characterized by giving itself away for God's kingdom or by seeking to "save" itself?

6. Is your church "kingdom" focused or "church" focused? Gives some reasons for your answer.

7. Is your church loving? In what ways?

CHAPTER THREE

Christ's Presence and His Church

CHRIST'S PRESENCE MAKES THE DIFFERENCE

Imagine you are at your church's business meeting. The news is not good. The church treasurer reports that offerings for the month were lower than anticipated. If she pays the mortgage, she will be unable to settle the bill for the new hot water tank and recent electrical work. If the trend continues, paying wages will be difficult. People begin a lively debate about the church's financial priorities.

The building and grounds committee chairman informs those present that the primary air conditioning units may not last the summer. The roof over the sanctuary needs repairs. An animated conversation commences questioning everything from why the church did not carry an extended warranty to whether a local roofing company would give the church a deal on shingles. The men's ministry leader says only three men attended the monthly pancake breakfast. He is considering putting the event on hold until more interest develops.

Suddenly, the room explodes with noise. The door to the auditorium bursts open and light floods the room. To everyone's amazement, Jesus Christ majestically enters. His hair is a brilliant white. His face shines so brightly it is blinding. A razor-sharp, two-edged sword protrudes from His mouth. His eyes blaze like fire. Everyone instantly falls to the ground in awe. Christ serenely makes His way to the front of the auditorium and sits down. In an authoritative voice, He says, "Continue."

Would the business meeting's tone suddenly change? Would there be any more arguing? Would people leave that gathering feeling positive or negative? There are no pessimists in Christ's presence! How could there be? He is the King of kings. *Nothing* is impossible for Him. That business meeting would be the most exciting, encouraging, upbeat gathering in that church's history. Why? Because the risen Christ was present, and His presence changes everything.

AN OPEN DOOR

The seven churches in Asia were concerned about their future. Powerful enemies were rising up against them. Some church leaders had already been martyred (Rev. 2:13). John, the last of Jesus' twelve disciples, was in exile. But the risen Christ had a message for them.

To the church in Pergamum, Christ declared He knew Satan's throne was in the city and that Antipas, a faithful witness, had been slain (Rev. 2:13). Yet Christ reminded them that He stood in their midst, armed with a sharp, two-edged sword that spoke pure truth that cut through all falsehood (Rev. 2:12).

To the church at Philadelphia, He announced, *"The Holy One, the True One, the One who has the key of David, who opens and no one will close, and closes and no one opens says: I know your works. Because you have limited strength, have kept My word, and have not denied My name, look, I have placed before you an open door that no one is able to close. Take note! I will make those from the Synagogue of Satan, who claim to be Jews and are not, but are lying—note this—I will make them come and bow down at your feet, and they will know that I have loved you"* (Rev. 3:7-9). The church at Philadelphia had few resources. Their city was filled with evil forces seeking to harm them. Yet Christ did not remove their enemies. Instead, He promised that His presence in their midst would sustain them. Christ said their enemies would *"know that I have loved you."* What a blessed thought. Christ can bless you so that even your enemies recognize His love for you.

The Philadelphians may have assumed they needed larger offerings and better security. But Christ assured them His presence would bring victory. An open door meant that the risen, all-powerful Christ was always available to them.

Christ the Victor is fully accessible to every church that recognizes their need for Him and turns to Him for help. Notice what Christ promised to the church at Laodicea: *"Listen! I stand at the door and knock. If anyone hears My voice and opens the door, I will come in to him and have dinner with him, and he with Me. The victor: I will give him the right to sit with Me on My throne, just as I also won the victory and sat down with My Father on His throne"* (Rev. 3:20-21).

Christians often think of that passage in connection with evangelism, but the words were written to a lukewarm church (Rev. 3:15- 16). Jesus gave them a picture of the risen Christ inviting each person to enjoy fellowship with Him. All the people needed to do was hear His knock and receive Him into their midst. History does not record if they ever did.

Can you imagine a church chatting so loudly, singing so boisterously, or arguing so vehemently that not one person heard Christ knocking on their front door? Churches are often disoriented to Christ's voice and oblivious to His presence, which is why the risen Christ concluded His message to each of the seven churches by urging, *"Anyone who has an ear should listen to what the Spirit says to the churches"* (Rev. 2:7, 11, 17, 29; 3:6, 13, 22).

Every church body is equipped with spiritual senses, though many have grown unaccustomed to using them. Even Jesus' own disciples, after witnessing His mighty miracles, were rebuked for failing to recognize God's activity. Jesus asked, *"Do you have eyes, and not see, and do you have ears, and not hear?"* (Mark 8:18). Christ's presence does a church little good if His people do not recognize when He is seeking their attention.

CHRIST IN HIS CHURCH

I have stood in some of the grandest cathedrals in the world. As I gazed at the stained-glass windows and vaulted ceilings, I could easily imagine Christ's presence in such a magnificent structure. But Christ is equally present in a thatched-roof church in rural Africa or a plain chapel in inner-city America. If churches recognize almighty God's presence in their midst, it revolutionizes their ministry.

I strived to teach my congregation this crucial truth. Our facility was one of the most unattractive buildings in the entire city. Our congregation was small. Our budget was meager. Our equipment was antiquated. Yet Christ's presence was just as available to us as to any church in the world. We just had to open the door.

When people heard about all God was doing through our church, they were often surprised to see how ordinary we were. A family once drove all the way from Oklahoma to attend our Sunday service. We had a delightful time of fellowship together, but they confessed that they were perplexed that a church accomplishing so much was so modest and small. I laughed and assured them that what was happening was due to God, not us. God was just as powerful in our midst as He was in the largest church in the world. We knew it and behaved like it, and that made all the difference.

The following are five of the profoundly practical differences Christ's presence makes in a church.

1. Christ's Presence Reflects a Relationship

One of the saddest indictments of today's church is that Christians often settle for religion rather than a relationship. Churches deteriorate into nothing more than religious institutions instead of the living, active body of Christ. Many churches have died because of this paradigm shift. Christ told the church at Laodicea that He stood at its door and desired to "... *come in to him, and have dinner with him*" (Rev. 3:20). In the ancient world, to share a meal with someone was to extend friendship. Meals were the primary way for people to open their lives up to others and enjoy their fellowship. The risen Christ desired not only the church's service, devotion, adherence, and belief but also its *fellowship*. He loved them and wanted a loving relationship with them.

The problem for many churches and some entire denominations is that people are disoriented to God. They hear a sermon or put their children in Sunday school, but no one helps them understand that Christ is seeking to relate to them personally.

When I preached, I alerted people that the Holy Spirit was in the room. I would say, "Some of you will sense a strange stirring in your heart. You will feel drawn to God. That is not my preaching. That is not the music. That is the Holy Spirit drawing you to Himself." At the close of the service, I would extend an invitation to anyone who wanted to come to the front of the sanctuary to speak with me or to pray. I promised to help them enter into a personal, loving relationship with the risen Christ. I did not ask them merely to pray the "sinner's prayer" or fill out a decision card. They were doing far more than joining an institution or making a public decision. They were entering into a personal, loving, dynamic relationship with almighty God.

Likewise, when people who were already believers asked to join our church, I made it clear that we were not just adding their names to our membership roll. Christ Himself was adding them to our church body (1 Cor. 12:18). Long before they made a public decision, the Holy Spirit was already drawing them to our church in preparation for the assignment he had for them there.

Adding someone's name to a membership roll is easy; accepting a new family member goes much deeper. If newcomers do not understand the covenant they are making with the church body, then when someone hurts their feelings or a more dynamic church opens down the street, they may choose to remove themselves from the roll. But if Christ adds believers to a church, only He can lead them away. It does not matter if the church replaces the pews in the auditorium with theater seating or if the worship team starts singing modern choruses or the pastor speaks about money too much. They have no right to leave the church in which God placed them. The church is a living body; it is not an institution.

Sometimes churches mistake worship services for a relationship with Christ. A beautifully lit, tastefully decorated auditorium can emulate the powerful presence of God. An emotional song can imitate the convicting work of the Holy Spirit. It is possible to come to church and experience a service rather than Christ. Yet there is no substitute for a personal encounter with the risen Lord.

When I first arrived in Saskatoon, our auditorium was extremely sparse. The tile floor was dull and chipped. We had cheap wooden and metal chairs. The piano and organ were of low quality. The sound system caused more problems than it solved. But week after week, people flooded the altar in tears after experiencing a fresh encounter with the living Christ. Services often ran long because people would spontaneously rise to share how deeply they had experienced Christ that day.

I doubt anyone joined our church because of our luxurious facility, cutting-edge music, or entertaining preaching. But people regularly shared how they felt compelled to join our fellowship because they encountered God every time they worshipped with us.

I have visited many small, struggling churches. The person making the announcements often says something like this: "I want to welcome those of you who are visiting. We have a lot of people away today, so our crowd is pretty small. We are glad you chose to come." They have it all wrong! Visitors do not come to encounter a large crowd; they come to experience God. Instead of emphasizing who is not there, point them to who is. A small church has as much of Christ to offer visitors as the massive cathedral downtown. Direct people's attention to Christ, who stands at the door of their life waiting to have fellowship with them!

The risen Christ did not limit His guidance to first-century churches. He intends to guide your church as well. Imagine the exalted Lord standing silently in your midst, never offering a word of comfort or counsel as you face difficult challenges. Impossible! He loves you too much to do that (Matt. 11:28-30).

The problem is that many of God's people are disoriented to Him. They fail to recognize His guidance. The Bible records centuries of interactions with God wherein He spoke to His people and gave specific instructions. The same God now directs your church

(John 16:7-15). He loves your church as much as He has loved any church in history. He knows how you can glorify Him. You will face problems too difficult to solve on your own. You must know how to recognize Christ's leading.

How will your church know what to do? Ask Him! Prayer is a conversation. When you pray, do not merely share your plans and ask God to bless them. Prayer is a time to listen. The risen Christ would say the same thing to many of today's churches that He said two thousand years ago: "... *listen to what the Spirit says to the churches.*"

2. Christ's Presence Brings Joy

The Psalmist declared, "... *In your presence is abundant joy; in your right hand are eternal pleasures*" (Ps. 16:11). Our church in Saskatoon had little to offer in terms of physical comforts or musical extravaganzas. The hard wooden chairs became painful when services ran long. The steady stream of amateurs leading worship sometimes produced unpleasant musical results. We did not have adequate parking. When winter temperatures plummeted to forty degrees below zero, walking three blocks from the nearest parking spot to the church building was not a pleasant experience. But we had joy. Why? Because we knew we would experience Christ at our church, and in His presence is *abundant* joy.

Joy is one of the best spiritual barometers for a church. When I visit a dying church, I rarely find joy. The announcements are monotone. The singing is halfhearted. The prayers are uninspired. I have seen church leaders look so long in the face it appeared they were attending a funeral rather than a worship service. Then, with a deadpan expression, they said, "I just don't know why no one wants to come to our church!" Joylessness almost assures that the church will eventually die. After all, most people find life hard enough without attending a depressing weekly worship service.

A church that lacks joy has lost its focus. It is impossible to gaze at the Son of Man of Revelation and remain unenthusiastic. But declining churches focused on their dwindling finances, small numbers, or deteriorating facilities tend to lose their joy. Christians who believe Christianity is just a set of doctrines or religious practices will not be joyful. They may be diligent, weary, and guilt-ridden, but they will not be overflowing with joy. When people understand that Christianity is about a loving, life-changing relationship with Christ, they will experience divine joy even amid difficult circumstances.

When I speak about the exciting work of God I witnessed through the years, I inevitably hear statements like, "Henry, I'm glad you saw God do so many amazing things in your ministry. But you have to understand, I'm in a difficult church." People often assume I stay positive because my ministry was candy-coated or easy. That is not the case. During my years as a pastor, I experienced obstacles and painful moments that could have crushed me had I not known the Lord's presence.

When we moved to Canada, the church was so poor it could not afford to pay for our move. We used our own funds. The church could offer only a meager salary, but they provided a modest parsonage. I had a family of seven, and the house had three tiny bedrooms and one bathroom. We were also expected to house summer missionaries and feed church guests in that humble abode. Eventually, some church members decided to add a bathroom in the basement of our house. Everyone agreed the addition was necessary. Then one member, the wealthiest man in the church, objected to the "unnecessary expense" of putting *walls* on the bathroom. After all, he argued, my four sons would occupy the basement. All they needed to do was hang blankets from the overhead beams.

That man could have single-handedly paid for all the renovations on the parsonage and never missed the money. Yet he preferred for the pastor's family to live in humiliating circumstances. How do you respond when people act selfishly? I hurried into God's presence. If Marilynn and I nursed resentment toward that man's profound lack of gratitude for all we had sacrificed, our joy would have evaporated. Instead, we turned to the Lord in whose right hand are "eternal pleasures." We have tried to make it a habit never to go to bed until we find something to laugh about. That evening was no different. We understood why God led us to that church: to help misguided, self-centered people like that man become a loving, joyful, Christ-honoring congregation. Our joy would not come from beautiful, four-walled bathrooms with upgraded fixtures but from the Lord's presence.

3. Christ's Presence Transforms Our Service

Serving Christ is an honor that should bring enormous joy and satisfaction. Yet when we take our eyes off of Jesus, serving Him can become drudgery and our efforts can actually dishonor Him (Luke 10:38-42). Most churches have members who serve in the church for the wrong reasons. They may cling to their position as a status symbol rather than as a means of expressing their gratitude to Christ. They may hold an office but bear little fruit (John 15:5). They may work hard but constantly complain about how unappreciated they are. They may faithfully show up to teach their Sunday school class or pass an offering plate, but no one ever sees them smile. This problem is exacerbated in declining churches as an increasing amount of work is distributed among fewer and fewer people. Unless people's eyes are riveted on Christ, serving Him can become a burden rather than a delight.

At the close of a revival service where I was a guest speaker, the Sunday school superintendent came forward and asked to receive Christ as his Savior. He tearfully confessed that he had started attending the church years earlier at his wife's prodding. He heard they needed helpers in the children's Sunday school area, so he volunteered. He eventually joined the church and ultimately became the superintendent of the Sunday school. Yet it seemed like God was not blessing his efforts. He worked hard but saw little spiritual fruit. That day, he finally realized the problem was not that he lacked volunteers or an ample budget but that he did not have a love relationship with Jesus. He was gloriously saved that day, and he began to experience the Holy Spirit's powerful equipping at last. Similar stories unfold frequently in churches across the land.

4. Christ's Presence Brings Peace

During the first two years I served in Saskatoon, it seemed as if circumstances conspired to stamp out our little congregation before we could accomplish anything for God's kingdom. My family arrived on the field in April. In December, Marilynn gave birth to our daughter, Carrie. Marilynn experienced severe complications after the birth.

I will never forget the night in the hospital when the surgeon gravely confessed, "I'm not sure we can save her." Marilynn was bleeding severely, and the doctors had been unable to stop it. That night I sat alone in the hospital waiting room. Someone from the church was at our home watching our children, but no one was at the hospital with me. We had left our fine church in California to minister in Saskatoon. We were destitute and had five children under the age of ten. My dear wife had joyfully agreed to leave her native country to serve alongside me in an extremely difficult setting, and it looked like I would lose her.

It was tempting to grow discouraged and quit. I had traversed 1,700 miles to encourage this church, but no one traveled four miles to sit with me in the hospital waiting room while I prepared to hear whether my wife would live. I had multiple seminary degrees and had experienced success at two previous churches, yet our church in Canada could not pay me a livable wage. I had left a secure pastorate to serve God in a mission setting, and it appeared my reward was to become an impoverished widower. Contemplating the future was bewildering.

But the Lord reminded me that I was *not* alone in the waiting room that evening. As I cried out to Him, He assured me that He loved me deeply. His tangible presence gave me peace, and I felt assured that Marilynn would recover. He affirmed that I was right where He wanted me to be. He had not released me from my assignment, regardless of how difficult it was. It is glorious when an entire room is permeated with God's peace (Phil. 4:6-7). I experienced God's presence that night. I rejoiced and worshipped Him. God had not removed the hardships from my life, but He was walking with me through them. I was confident He would see me through to the other side.

God does some of His greatest work when I am in my weakest state (2 Cor. 12:9-10). Marilynn recovered and has faithfully labored beside me many years since. Our five children ultimately felt God calling them into full-time Christian ministry. Our baby daughter became a missionary in Germany. Our church grew, prospered, and brought me much joy through the years. Christ's presence made all the difference. I could lose my money, my health, my job, and even my wife, but no one could remove Christ's presence from me.

5. Christ's Presence Brings Focus

If I asked you whether Christ was present in your church, you would probably affirm that He was. But what if I asked you what practical difference Christ's presence made in how your church functions? Although we know the theologically correct response, many churches have never truly experienced Christ's presence in their midst.

As a young pastor, I learned that asking the wrong question elicits the wrong response. For example, I was misleading my flock if I asked, "What do you think we should do?" The key was not people's opinion but God's will. It was better to ask, "As you have been praying and seeking Christ's will on this matter, what has He revealed to you?" When I posed that question, two things happened. First, those who were not praying and seeking God's will were often silenced. They may have had plenty of opinions on financial and administrative issues, but they had not taken time to discover God's opinion, so they were unprepared to voice their thoughts. Second, people who had prayed and sought answers in Scripture would burst forth with truth and wisdom from above.

If I asked our core members at the Wednesday evening prayer meeting, "What did you think of last Sunday?" I might hear, "Attendance was down last week," or "Offerings were awfully low. I hope they pick up before the end of the month." But if I asked, "What did you see God doing in the service last Sunday?" I would get an entirely different response. Someone might say, "It was so good to see Randy in the service last week! Many of us have been praying for him, and God is clearly drawing him to Himself," or "I saw Roger serving as an usher last week. He has been an extremely shy person all of his life. It is great to see how God is giving him confidence to serve in our church!" Notice how the focus changes.

Some people have told me, "You are an *optimist*, but I am a *realist*." The implication is that I am naively positive, whereas they see the harsh reality of the circumstances. But there is *nothing* more "real" than Christ's presence in His church. Sure, offerings might be low, attendance may have dipped, and perhaps no one chose to join the church last Sunday. Yet all of those concerns must be placed beside the most important truth: *"The risen Christ is present in His church!"* Every other observation ought to be viewed in light of that preeminent reality.

I served as the moderator for our church business meetings. Those gatherings led to some of our most spiritually profound moments as we identified practical ways Christ was guiding us and providing for our needs. I instructed committee chairpersons to deliver their report in light of the fact that Christ was triumphantly ruling on His throne. The finance person would not merely disclose expenses and bottom lines but also help us celebrate God's provision and alert us to areas that required our faith. The missions pastor would not simply report what our mission teams had done the previous month. He would also share where he saw God working and celebrate how the Lord of the harvest continued to thrust forth laborers. Each report focused more on Christ's activity than on ours. It is exhilarating when a church operates with the understanding that Christ rules in the midst of His people.

6. Christ's Presence Brings Accountability

One difference Christ's presence makes in the church becomes evident when we sin. When Christ examined the seven churches, He did not say to the church at Ephesus, "Your love for me has grown cold. Try harder to love Me more!" No! He said, *"Repent!"* (Rev. 2:5). When the risen Christ viewed the church at Pergamum, He did not say, "You need to make some adjustments in how you receive members who are followers of the teachings of Balaam or the Nicolaitans." He said, *"Repent!"* (Rev. 2:16). Christ also told the churches at Thyatira, Sardis, and Laodicea to repent (Rev. 2:21; 3:3, 19). Why? Because they had not just been careless or become too busy. They had sinned against almighty God. The only remedy for sin is repentance.

Churches like to minimize sin. Perhaps one member becomes angry at another member and leaves the church. She says many unkind things about the church and refuses to forgive the person who offended her. Later, when she cools off and returns, the church breathes a sigh of relief and carries on as if nothing happened. But that church member did not just "blow off some steam." She sinned against a holy God, and she needs to repent. Quite likely, so does the person who offended her. Church members do not simply get too busy to spend time with God. They forsake meeting with their Savior. They need to repent. People do not merely fail to follow through on their commitment to the church. They break their promise to God. They do not need to rededicate their life. They need to repent.

If Christianity were just a matter of being religious, churches could try harder. But because churches are accountable to Christ, we must repent of our sin when we forsake Him. What did Christ tell you to do? Obey Him!

One day we will give an account to Christ for our actions, both good and bad (2 Cor. 5:10). On that day, comments that offended us will no longer matter. It will make no difference whether anyone thanked us. In that moment, Christ will ask, "Did you do what I asked you to do?"

◢ CONCLUSION

Our church learned that Christ's presence was not just a theological doctrine; it was a practical reality. Because Christ was present, we did not have to fret about finances. Because our Lord walked among us, we had no reason to be anxious about the challenges we faced. Because Christ was with us, we could enter the future with confidence. Christ's presence changed everything. His presence will make all the difference for you too.

◢ QUESTIONS FOR REFLECTION

1. Is your church Christ-focused? What are three practical differences being Christ-focused makes in how your church functions?

2. Does your church practice religion or are you enjoying a love relationship with the risen Christ? What evidence supports your answer?

3. Is your church characterized by the joy of the Lord?

4. Does your church make decisions based on Christ's presence in your midst? Provide an example.

5. How is church business reported to the congregation? Is the focus on problems or on Christ?

6. Are people in your church being held accountable to Christ for their actions? In what ways?

7. How does your church encourage people to repent when they sin against God? How might your church's attitude toward sin impact God's blessing on your church?

◤ CHAPTER FOUR

Christ's Power and His Church

GOD'S POWER, DAY BY DAY

Throughout my decades of ministry, I have learned some important lessons about God's power. First, it does not take a miracle to live in disobedience, but His power becomes indispensable as soon as you start to obey. Second, God's power is most often evident in life's ordinary moments. At times, I witnessed God accomplish the miraculous. More often, I experienced God's might in the course of ordinary undertakings, such as rearing five children in an impoverished church setting or driving thousands of miles on icy roads to do mission work. One thing is certain: once you experience God's power in your life and ministry, you will never want to live or serve without it again.

I also learned that as soon as you choose to obey God, you will inevitably hear a host of reasons why you should not! After our church agreed to sponsor the mission church in Prince Albert, I was inundated with cautionary advice. People asked whether I had ever driven in a Saskatchewan blizzard. They told me how wind could drive the snow from the fields across the highway and create a "white out," which severely impacted visibility. Black ice would gather on the highway and blend in with the blacktop. A car could hit a patch of ice at sixty miles an hour and spin out of control. Temperatures in the winter often dipped to fifty degrees below zero. The "wind chill" made conditions even worse. Everyone seemed eager to share a story of a hapless traveler who had frozen to death while stranded in his vehicle. I quickly discovered that the "winter jacket" I had brought with me from southern California was woefully inadequate for Saskatchewan weather. To make matters worse, I had brought a Volkswagen bus with me from California that was definitely not designed for arctic conditions! The heater never worked well, and the vehicle struggled to run in subzero temperatures. Yet when well-meaning church members warned me about the winter storms, my response was always the same: "If Jesus could calm a storm on the Sea of Galilee, I'm sure He can overcome a blizzard in Saskatchewan!"

I concluded that if God told our church to do something, He would provide whatever was necessary for us to obey. For the first two years I lived in Saskatoon, I led services in Prince Albert every Sunday afternoon and Tuesday evening. Neither weather conditions nor vehicle malfunctions ever prevented me from going (although at times my Volkswagen seemed to be powered more by prayer than by gasoline).

The greatest challenge for me was the cost to my family. Marilynn's health broke after the birth of our fifth child. She carried a heavy load both physically and emotionally while I was away. One Tuesday afternoon, I stopped at the edge of town to call Marilynn from a gas station before I entered the highway for Prince Albert. She was crying. The burden was too much. I returned home, and we wept together. We knew God had called us to do missions in Canada, but the load seemed too great to bear at times. We cried out to God for help. The Holy Spirit infused our little home with peace. Marilynn said, "Henry, you can go now. I'll be all right. I know this is what God wants us to do. I just needed you for a little while."

One Tuesday I drove alone to Prince Albert. No one showed up to the meeting. The Lord and I had a special time that evening as I drove the hour and a half back home. There were many such moments in those early years when Marilynn and I could have easily grown discouraged and quit. Each time, the Lord made His powerful presence extremely real to us, and we experienced His peace and joy.

We often long for spectacular displays of God's infinite power in our church. We wish He would miraculously remove all our problems or send us an enormous financial gift. But most of the time God's power is evident in the steady grind of ordinary living as we faithfully obey the last thing He told us to do.

RULERS OF CLAY

If someone in the first century were asked to think of a powerful person, the Roman emperor likely would have come to mind. With thousands of seemingly invincible legionaries and the enormous wealth of the empire at his disposal, no human being exercised more might than the emperor did. During Emperor Nero's reign, Christians were thrown to wild dogs or dipped in wax and lit on fire to illuminate his gardens at night. Yet Nero's armies eventually turned against him, and he begged his servant to kill him before his enemies reached him. Tradition claims that John wrote the Book of Revelation during Emperor Domitian's reign. Though he was considered the most powerful person in the world, Domitian ultimately died an ignoble death at the hands of one of his servants. The world's most powerful people have repeatedly proven to be mere creatures of clay.

A TIMELY WORD

Government officials exiled John to the remote island of Patmos (Rev. 1:9). Every day John spent in that desolate place reminded him that there were people in his world with powers far greater than his own. The Christian community knew they were vulnerable to the wicked plots of governments, tyrants, and evil people. Perhaps that is why Christ personally visited John and gave him an inspiring word for the churches. Christ could have sent an angel to deliver His message. He could have dictated the book of *Revelation* into John's consciousness. But the risen Christ chose to impress upon John and the Early Church the glory and power of the One who offered them hope.

John walked with Jesus for more than three years. He sat next to Jesus during the Last Supper (John 13:25). He cared for Jesus' mother (John 19:26-27). John had experienced Christ as a friend, teacher, counselor, savior, and master. He had observed firsthand his Lord's mastery over nature, sickness, demons, and death. Yet when John saw the Lord in His glorified, exalted state, he was overwhelmed. Though John had witnessed Jesus' transfiguration, he had never encountered Christ in this terrifying way. His voice was as loud as cascading waters. His face shone as brightly as the sun. From His mouth came a razor-sharp sword. Christ described Himself as "*... the Alpha and the Omega... the One who is, who was, and who is coming, the Almighty*" (Rev. 1:8). Christ went on to assure John, "*I am the First and the Last, and the Living One. I was dead, but look—I am alive forever and ever, and I hold the keys of death and Hades*" (Rev. 1:17-18). Given the magnificent appearance of the risen Savior, it is no wonder John trembled at the encounter!

Revelation provides spectacular imagery, but clearly John's human vocabulary was inadequate to describe the glorified Christ who stood before him. How can a mortal tongue satisfactorily recount a divine encounter? One day we will stand before that same Christ, and we too will be overwhelmed by the sight. Then we will fully understand the word "hallelujah."

CHRIST AND HIS CHURCHES

When John saw Christ in His exalted state, how could he or his readers doubt that their Lord had the solution to every one of their problems? Christ's infinite power was manifested to the churches in the following ways:

- The Ephesians had grown cold in their devotion to their Lord, but God's powerful grace was sufficient to restore them to a deep, abiding love.

- The church at Smyrna faced tribulation and imprisonment, yet Christ's sustaining power would bring them through the worst their enemies could do to them and ultimately grant them victory.

- The church at Pergamum was tolerating false doctrine, but Christ could infuse those believers with a vigorous passion for truth.

- The church at Thyatira was condoning sexual immorality, but Christ in His awesome wrath was preparing to punish the evildoers severely, even to the point of death.

- The church at Sardis had a reputation for spiritual vibrancy, but the Lord was not deceived. He would expose their hypocrisy and bring judgment upon those who refused to repent.

- The church at Philadelphia was under attack by evil spiritual forces. Christ extended His mighty hand in order to humiliate their enemies, protect them, and offer them constant access to His holy presence.

- The church at Laodicea had become wealthy and prideful. Christ warned them about their complacency; He would severely humble them in order to reinforce their dependence on Him.

The seven churches in Asia all had serious needs and problems. Some were of their own making, while others were the result of persecution. Christ left no doubt that He could meet their needs, defeat their opponents, protect them from danger, deal with their sin, and restore their spiritual passion.

The churches' problems became an opportunity for Christ to put His power on display.

ALL THINGS ARE POSSIBLE

As a pastor, I faced a crisis of belief. I asked, "Is the reason small churches experience so little of God's power because God does not work powerfully through small congregations or merely because they *assume* He will not?" 1 Corinthians 1:27 states, *"Instead, God has chosen the world's foolish things to shame the wise, and God has chosen the world's weak things to shame the strong."* We certainly qualified as weak! Rather than bemoaning our small size and many frailties, we had the opportunity to showcase what God could do through an ordinary group of people who believed that all things are possible with God.

The challenge for us as a church was to put that belief into action. Many Christians affirm God's omnipotence as a doctrine; fewer practice it as a lifestyle. Our church's constitution included a statement about God's power; I wanted to incorporate that belief into our calendar, budget, worship services, and prayer meetings. We claimed God was almighty, yet we were not attempting to do what only God could do.

One of the verses that guided us was Hebrews 11:6: *"Now without faith it is impossible to please God ..."* God is pleased by *faith*, not *self-sufficiency*. For our church to please God, we had to walk by faith. Ironically, churches constantly work to *eliminate* the need for faith by developing budgets and stockpiling cash reserves. While those practices might make financial sense, they do not signify faith.

Which pattern of behavior do you think will draw a watching world to Christ: a congregation that is tentative and cautious, only endeavoring what it can afford, or a church that is accomplishing feats that can only be explained by God?

Unbelievers will be drawn to Christ when they see Him acting miraculously through a local church. How do I know? Because that is what we experienced.

GOD'S POWER ON DISPLAY

Statistics on American churches are alarming. Roughly 70% of congregations are plateaued or in decline. Thousands of churches have not seen a single conversion in more than a year. Long-time members faithfully attend and serve each week, yet the worship is lifeless. No one expresses excitement for the future. Few anticipate God accomplishing anything unusual in their midst.

Misrepresenting Christ is an affront to almighty God, but churches do it all the time. Churches are Christ's body to their community, yet they grow discouraged and display an anemic faith. People see a weak church and assume it serves a weak God. Churches may have little power of their own, but they ought to behave like servants of an all-powerful King (Ex. 14:13-18).

The psalmist Asaph declared, *"We must not hide them from their children, but must tell a future generation the praises of the Lord, His might, and the wonderful works He has performed"* (Ps. 78:4). Asaph wanted the next generation to learn about God's awesome works. Today's church ought to desire the same thing.

Children who grew up attending church are leaving the faith in droves once they graduate from high school. Why? Because they never experienced God's power in their church. They listened to adults discuss mundane organizational issues like programming and potlucks. Perhaps they overheard gossip about other church members or arguments in business meetings, but they rarely, if ever, heard God's name exalted. They sang hymns like "A Mighty Fortress Is Our God" and then watched as church members reacted fearfully to demographic shifts in their community. They listened to Sunday school lessons on Shadrach, Meshach, and Abednego's fearless commitment to truth and then heard their church leaders discuss how to behave in a more politically correct fashion. They learned about missionaries in far-flung nations laying their life down for the cause of Christ and then observed adults angrily debate the pros and cons of allowing an ethnic congregation to use the church's facility on Sunday afternoons.

Many of these young people grew up in churches that acted feebly, and they have no desire to spend the remainder of their lives propping up the institution like their parents did.

I suspect that our humble church building made it easier for young people to draw near to Christ. Many told me that since we had no stained glass, vaulted ceilings, or pipe organs, they felt less intimidated about attending our services. What some viewed as a weakness, God used as a strength. As a result, we had a steady stream of hurting, broken, and confused people walk through our door.

I never felt like my children missed out on anything because they grew up in a small church. Sure, they never had a full-time youth minister, young adult trips to the beach, or a recreation center. But they saw God display His life-changing power.

When Marilynn and I encountered people who were experiencing God's power, we invited them to join us for a meal. College students who had been expelled from their parents' house for sharing their faith joined us for the holidays. Pastors and volunteers who traveled great distances to serve with us spent time in our home. When our church received funding, we told our children of God's gracious provision. More than once, Mariynn and I found an alcoholic passed out in the front yard of our house. We would usher him into our home and encourage him to take a shower while Marilynn prepared a hot meal and washed his clothes. Our children never knew who might be joining us for dinner or how thinly we might have to slice the dessert that evening, but they continually witnessed the amazing work God was doing in the midst of our little church.

OPEN YOUR EYES!

For the church at Ephesus, Paul prayed that *"the eyes of your heart may be enlightened so you may know... what is the immeasurable greatness of His power to us who believe, according to the working of His vast strength... And He put everything under His feet and appointed Him as Head over everything for the church, which is His body..."* (Eph. 1:18-19, 22). The problem is not that small churches have few resources but that many churches fail to recognize the enormous power that is readily at their disposal. If churches opened their spiritual eyes to the immensity of God's power that is fully available to them, we would experience revival.

Our church had spent too many years focusing on what it could or could not do. I taught people to look for where God was already working in our midst. Whenever we recognized God's activity, we joined Him.

The following are six observations about how almighty God chooses to work among His people.

1. Christ Draws People to Himself

Jesus declared, *"For the Son of Man has come to save the lost"* (Matt. 18:11). Saving the lost is Christ's heart, and it should be the church's driving passion too. But how can a church translate that desire into action?

Marketing techniques attract crowds, but only God can draw people to His Son. Scripture teaches, *"... There is no one righteous, not even one. There is no one who understands; there is no one who seeks God"* (Rom. 3:10-11). Sin separated us from God, and we cannot find our way back to Him in our own strength. Yet Jesus promised, *"As for Me, if I am lifted up from the earth I will draw all people, to Myself"* (John 12:32).

By now you know that our little church could not entice people with a beautiful facility, celebrity-riddled membership, or cutting-edge music.

Our facility was an eyesore. Our membership included a wide assortment of ordinary people ranging from casually dressed university students to recovering alcoholics. We welcomed a strong contingent of people with mental and physical disabilities. Our members included widows, immigrants, young couples, and social misfits. There were no bank managers, CEOs, government officials, or high-profile community leaders. From the outset, we were keenly aware that people would join us only if God drew them.

During one Sunday evening service, I invited people to share what God was doing in their life. A college student who had recently started attending our services asked to speak. He explained that he felt drawn to our church and had started reading his Bible. I recognized that he was not yet a believer. There, in front of the entire church family that evening, I helped him pray to receive Christ as his Lord and Savior. Our congregation was thrilled to witness Christ draw someone to Himself. Similar stories unfolded again and again. Each time, we recognized Christ's activity. We felt humbled that the Lord chose to use our church to reach unbelievers in our city.

2. Christ Transforms People

Not only did we witness God save people from their sin but we also saw Christ radically transform lives by His grace.

The apostle Paul was once a fierce enemy of the church. Yet Christ saved him from his sin and transformed him into a saint. Paul declared, *"But by God's grace I am what I am, and His grace toward me was not ineffective... "* (1 Cor. 15:10). Our church show-cased numerous people Christ had freed from sin and transformed into men and women of God.

Many of the people who came to our church had been deeply hurt earlier in their life. Some had been sexually assaulted. Others were addicted to drugs or alcohol. Several had been ensnared by the occult. Sometimes during Bible studies, college students would become so excited about what they were learning that they would express themselves using profanity. Young ladies would "dress up" for church in the same outfits they previously wore to bars. We learned never to be surprised by who entered our sanctuary. We were thrilled to see Christ drawing people to Himself. We knew He would not only free them from the bondage of their past, but He would also transform them into ambassadors of grace.

Gerry was one of those college students. He had long hair and indulged in many of the sins popular with young people at that time. He had no direction for his life and was desperately searching for meaning and purpose. I watched Christ take hold of Gerry's life. Soon, he approached me and described his new passion to serve God. Was there a place he could minister? I told him about an indigenous congregation 85 miles away from our church. Their pastor was growing older and needed help. Gerry volunteered to go. Each Sunday, he drove his rattletrap vehicle to that community so he could labor alongside the veteran minister. When the pastor's health forced him to retire, the church members asked Gerry to take his place. Gerry moved on-site and became their full-time minister.

As he led that small flock, he was inspired to finish his university degree. Over the next few years, he pastored and planted churches while completing his bachelor's program. Later he felt led to enroll in seminary, so he and his wife Connie (a young lady who came to Christ through our college ministry) and their two daughters moved to San Francisco. As a seminary student, he pastored a congregation. When he completed his seminary training, he returned to Canada. Having been reared in a French-Canadian family, Gerry was bilingual. He moved to the province of Quebec, where he worked to reach French-speaking people for Christ

Today, he is the National Ministry Leader for his denomination in Canada, and he is leading an initiative to plant 1,000 new churches across the nation. I had the privilege of baptizing Gerry, ordaining him, and performing his wedding. I watched God transform him into a wonderful man of God. Gerry's three adult children are now actively at work in church planting and young adult ministry.

Gerry's story is one of dozens I could tell of the beautiful, redeeming work God performed in and through the people He brought to Faith Baptist Church. Each one testified to God's power to take the most sin-scarred, damaged life and construct a monument to His infinite love.

3. Christ Rules the Nations

When I left California to serve in Canada, I was well aware that the northern nation had a reputation for being a difficult place to grow a church. The government was extremely secular and often passed laws that went against the values and beliefs of our church. The percentage of the national population who professed to be Christians had been plummeting for years. Many denominations and churches were in decline. Numerous pastors and denominational leaders in Canada warned me that I could not expect God to work in my church in Canada the same way he had in the United States. The oft-repeated refrain was, "It's different in Canada."

I would be quick to acknowledge that Canadians are different from Americans, and there are unique challenges to growing churches in Canada. But I refused to believe that God's power somehow ebbed when it reached the forty-ninth parallel. I realized God had just as much power in Canada as He did in any other nation. Our church chose to cling to that truth, and our behavior demonstrated our faith.

Many churches today have grown discouraged by their government's actions. When secular politicians pass laws that violate biblical standards, some congregations worry and fret. Small churches with little political, economic, or legal clout are particularly susceptible to that fear. The book of Psalms offers some perspective: "*Why do the nations rebel and the peoples plot in vain? The kings of the earth take their stand and the rulers conspire together against the Lord and His Anointed One: 'Let us tear off their chains and free ourselves from their restraints.' The One enthroned in heaven laughs; the Lord ridicules them*" (Psalm 2:1-4).

Our tiny church recognized that we had little legal or political power of our own. There were no government officials or powerful corporate CEOs among our members. The Canadian government constantly promoted "political correctness." We had nowhere to turn but to the Lord for guidance and protection. We also had to trust that regardless of how "difficult" our nation's religious climate might be, God was powerful enough to accomplish a great work through our modest congregation. Our focus had to remain on Christ, not the government.

When you put your hope in people or government leaders, you will inevitably be disappointed. If you keep your eyes riveted on Christ, He will constantly amaze you! Over the years, God used our ordinary congregation to reach students at an extremely secular university. God led our church to infuse Christian values into the public school system's English curriculum. God even enabled one of our mission pastors to be elected to parliament. God showed us that despite being small and financially weak, we need not fear any government, court, or law. Our God was sovereign over every nation. The key was to listen to Him rather than worrying about what law the government might enact.

God also convinced us that He wanted to use our church to impact the nations. As people in our church learned of God's love for the world, they willingly volunteered to travel around the globe and share the gospel. Two doctors went to the Middle East to serve in mission hospitals. College students committed to serving their Lord internationally. It was marvelous to see how God used a little church on the prairies of western Canada to touch the world.

4. God Rules the Economy

Sometimes churches fixate on the world's activity rather than on God's. We can be more concerned with interest rates or contingency funds than with God's will. When the economy fluctuates, it is easy to get sidetracked by financial "what ifs." We can become intimidated by bankers, government rules, or hostile city councils that seem intent on hindering God's work. Our church learned that regardless of how dismal our situation appeared, God could orchestrate any circumstances for our good.

At one point our church was seeking financing to expand our facility, and we were waiting on funds to be forwarded to us from a lending agency in the United States. We needed the loan to proceed with the project, but we experienced continual delays. It seemed to many that our church's progress was in the hands of a bureaucrat in a foreign financial institution. Some wondered if we were making a mistake. After weeks of setbacks, the situation appeared bleak. Nevertheless, I encouraged our congregation to trust that our church was in the hands of God, not in the palm of a banker.

Then one day, for just a few hours, the value of the Canadian currency plummeted dramatically compared to the American dollar. It was during those few hours that our funds were suddenly processed. Because the exchange rate had altered so significantly, our church received tens of thousands of dollars more than we would have if the money had been sent when we expected it. Soon after we deposited the money, the value of the Canadian dollar returned to its normal rate.

We were humbled and grateful. From a human perspective, we appeared to be but hapless victims of financial institutions and government regulations. But God proved once again who was sovereign over banks, businesses, and bureaucrats. Our hope was never in a favorable government or a sympathetic banker but in the Lord our God (Ps. 145:18).

5. Christ Brings in the Harvest

After I arrived in Canada, a Christian organization released a study indicating that Canada needed 10,000 new churches if every Canadian were to have a reasonable opportunity to hear the gospel. As our church studied our province, we found town after town sorely in need of a church. Clearly, the mission field was enormous. But our small congregation was barely able to staff our own Sunday school program, let alone provide pastors for the churches our nation urgently needed.

Jesus commanded, *"The harvest is abundant, but the workers are few. Therefore, pray to the Lord of the harvest to send out workers into His harvest"* (Matt. 9:37- 38). In light of this Scripture passage, we believed God would provide all the laborers we needed if we beseeched Him to bring them forward. In fact, the harvesters were plentiful; it was just that many of them were, as yet, non-Christians attending the local university. So we ministered to students and watched to see who Christ drew to Himself.

Over the twelve years I served as a pastor in Saskatoon, we saw God call more than 100 people into Christian ministry. During that time, I heard many long-time pastors complain that Canadians did not respond easily to a "call to ministry." In fact, many veteran pastors I knew had never had a single church member respond to a call into a Christian vocation. I noticed in Scripture that Christ first called people to Himself and *then* He sent them out on mission. My role as the pastor was not necessarily to "call out the called" but to lead people into an intimate, obedient relationship with their Lord. Then they would clearly hear and respond to whatever assignment the Lord gave them. Many people have expressed amazement at how many people felt God's call on their life over the course of my ministry. But it does not surprise me. I simply taught people that God doesn't draw us to Himself merely so we can receive a blessing; He calls us to Himself so we can be on mission (Matt. 10:1).

This truth became profoundly personal to me when I sensed God had a special purpose for each of my children. When my oldest son, Richard, was born, God impressed on me that He would use Richard in Christian ministry. I never told my son what God had revealed to me out of concern that he might enter the ministry simply because his dad thought he should. Instead, I prayed to the Lord of the harvest. When Richard became a teenager, my faith was sorely tested! Richard went through some difficult years during which he experienced pressure and even persecution for being a Christian. As he got older, I sensed he was running from the Lord because he was afraid of what yielding to God might cost him. At times, I wanted to intervene and explain to Richard God's plans for his life. But I did not.

One Sunday morning, I extended an altar call at the close of the service. Suddenly, I saw Richard make his way towards me. He tearfully confessed he had been running from God, but he could resist no longer. There, at the front of the church, I told my son that I had always known he was called into ministry. "Why didn't you tell me that?" he asked. "Because I wanted you to hear it from God first," I answered.

Before I dismissed the congregation, I asked Richard to share with his church family what God was doing in his life. Embarrassed and wiping away tears, Richard quickly explained that he had fully surrendered to what he knew was God's will for him: full-time ministry. I was drawing the service to a close when another student suddenly spoke up. He confessed that he, too, had been resisting God's will, but he was now prepared to submit. Then another young man stood up and shared how he also felt God's call on his life. By the time we dismissed, a dozen people had come to the altar to pray and commit themselves to the Lord's service.

Richard graduated from university and went on to earn two degrees from seminary. He served as a pastor and then as president of a seminary for thirteen years. Today he is the president of Blackaby Ministries International (www.blackaby.org). It has been my joy to speak with him around the world and to co-author numerous books with him. Each of my children underwent a similar experience, and each one is serving the Lord faithfully today. I learned that I could trust the Lord of the harvest, even when He was calling my own children to labor in the fields.

6. God Protects His People

There are dozens of ways I could illustrate how God's power made a dramatic difference in our church, but let me mention just one more—God's protection.

My family and I experienced God's providential care for us on numerous occasions. When we had been in Saskatoon for only one month, Marilynn got up in the middle of the night and walked straight into an intruder who was entering our bedroom. God blessed my wife with an amazing set of lungs, which she used to their fullest extent at that moment. Miraculously, no one was harmed, though I suspect that poor thief heard a ringing in his ears for days afterward.

Several years later, three of our sons traveled seven hours to attend a student winter retreat. They were scheduled to return home Sunday afternoon.

Shortly before two-thirty that afternoon, Marilynn urgently approached me and exclaimed, "We need to pray for the boys!" We knelt side by side and fervently prayed for our sons' safety. When they finally pulled into our driveway, Marilynn hurried out to their vehicle and asked how their trip had been. They reported that at two-thirty that afternoon, their car had hit a patch of black ice. The vehicle began spinning wildly down the middle of the undivided highway. An 18-wheel truck was barreling straight for them at 60 miles per hour. Suddenly, the tires of their car caught dry pavement and jerked backwards into the ditch on the right side of the highway. Just a few seconds longer and they would have collided with the truck. They all would have certainly perished. I do not understand the mysterious workings of prayer or why God so clearly prompted us to intercede on that occasion, but Marilynn and I once again experienced God's powerful hand working out His purposes in our church and family.

Though we faced break-ins and winter storms, our most painful experiences involved other Christians. When we began starting mission churches, we often received criticism from sister churches who had never begun a mission church themselves. Some felt we were trying to make a name for ourselves or, worse yet, trying to make other churches look bad. It amazed me that our church received more ridicule for coming back to life than we did when we were dying!

At the height of God's work in our church, we received our most grievous assaults. One pastor in our association drove to the United States and discouraged churches from funding our mission work. Another pastor wrote letters to our supporters, lying about our work and misrepresenting our efforts. A third pastor sought to undermine support for the Bible college our church was operating. We began to receive word from various churches that they would no longer be supporting our mission work. Our college was removed from several organizations' budgets. When people in our church learned what was happening, they were bewildered. How could God allow ungodly, petty people to cause such damage to a work we knew He had initiated? One of my sons came to me and asked why I was not refuting those pastors and exposing their actions to our denomination.

That was a critical time for me as a minister and for our church. We had faithfully sought to obey what God told us to do.

Yet rather than encouraging or even ignoring us, people were expressing anger toward us. Had we made a mistake? Should we confront our critics?

We believed the doctrine that God was all-powerful. In those difficult moments, we needed to let that belief guide our actions. I shared two verses with my church family that had greatly comforted me. The first came from 1 Samuel 2:30: "... *I will honor those who honor Me, but those who despise Me will be disgraced.*" I explained that when I began following Jesus, I gave Him my reputation. It belonged to Him, and He could do with it whatever He chose. I would not spend my time running around trying to protect my name. It was not people's opinions that mattered but God's. The greatest danger we faced as a church was not threats from our critics but the temptation to shift our focus from God to people.

The second Scripture came from Daniel 3:17-18: "*If the God we serve exists, then He can rescue us from the furnace of blazing fire, and He can rescue us from the power of you, the king. But even if He does not rescue us, we want you as king to know that we will not serve your gods or worship the gold statue you set up.*" Shadrach, Meshach, and Abednego had been attacked by ungodly enemies and faced a cruel, unjust death. Yet their belief in God's power never wavered. They declared their conviction that God could deliver them. Then they stated that *even if He did not*, their trust in Him would not falter. I referenced Daniel 3:17 on my business cards: "*Our God whom we serve is able... and He will ...*" As a church, we determined to continuing obeying God and leave the results to Him.

What happened next was sobering. All three of those pastors experienced horrendous circumstances in their personal lives. All three ultimately left the ministry. All three of those men's marriages were painfully shaken, with one ending in divorce. Some of their children suffered greatly. I was reminded that Scripture declares, *"It is a terrifying thing to fall into the hands of the living God"* (Heb. 10:31). We experienced first-hand that God's power was more than adequate to protect us from those who sought to harm us.

As time passed, people began to recognize that God was working mightily in our church. People traveled from all over the land to witness what God was doing. Pastors who had experienced discouragement joined our church family to receive healing and support. Never forget: regardless of how small or weak your church may be, *anything* is possible in the hands of almighty God.

◢ QUESTIONS FOR REFLECTION

1. Is your church currently behaving according to the reality that Christ is the all-powerful Lord of the universe? If so, list three examples. If not, list three changes you could make.

2. How is God's power being demonstrated in the way He is drawing people to Himself through your church?

3. Is God transforming lives through your church? List several examples.

4. How is God using your church to impact the nations?

5. Is God's power evident in the way He is thrusting forth laborers from your church? If not, why?

6. How are you seeing God's power demonstrated in the way He is protecting your church? If you are not currently experiencing God's power, what changes might you make?

7. Carefully read through Revelation 1 and Isaiah 40. Is your church currently functioning according to the truths portrayed in these Scriptures? If not, what adjustments must you make?

CHAPTER FIVE

Christ's Provision and His Church

JACK CONNER MOVED BY FAITH

Every time God places you in a position of need, He enables you to experience His provision. During my time in Saskatoon, God made it abundantly clear that we could approach Him whenever we lacked something. When I moved to Canada, the worship leader from my former church and his family of five came with us. A ten-person church that had almost died called two pastors with families totaling 12 members! Well-meaning friends asked how I intended to feed my children, let alone send them to college. I can testify that it was exhilarating to experience God's practical, loving, even humorous provision for our every need.

Two years after my arrival, the church in Prince Albert sensed it was time to call a full-time pastor. God led them to Jack Conner. Jack and I had been prayer partners as seminary students. He was a man of enormous faith and integrity. He was also the pastor of a thriving church in California that was seeing many people come to Christ. I knew Jack would be undaunted by the challenges of developing that mission church and that he would trust God to start missions across the northern regions of the province. Yet we faced an immediate challenge of gathering enough funds to cover Jack's salary and moving costs.

I always found it easier to make a sacrifice myself than to ask someone else to make one. I had moved to Canada by faith two years earlier, and we had experienced God's provision. It was more difficult for me to ask my friend to relocate his family to a challenging assignment. Yet Jack was such a man of faith that before we even officially invited him to come or knew how we would pay his salary, he sold his house and prepared to move.

We prayed for God to provide Jack's income, just as He had mine. Churches and individuals began responding, promising to send regular funds to cover Jack's salary.

On the day Jack and his family were scheduled to arrive at my home, we had pledges to cover his first year's salary, but we did not have any funds set aside for his moving expenses. I received a call from First Baptist Church in Fayetteville, Arkansas. They had collected a missions offering and were sending us $1,500, a very generous and unexpected gift in the 1970s. As I hung up the phone, Jack pulled into our driveway with his family. When I asked him how much his move had cost, he replied, "Henry, as best I can tell, it came to $1,500."

Over time, our little church learned that God was faithful to provide for our every need as we *obeyed Him*. Timing was key. In my experience, faith is always linked to action. It does not take faith to believe God can provide for your needs. It requires faith to resign from a good job, sell your house, and relocate your family 1,700 miles before you know if your new employer can even cover the cost of your gas and lodging. The apostle James wrote; "*Foolish man! Are you willing to learn that faith without works is useless?*" (James 2:20).

Faith is not expressed by what we say but by what we do. After decades of ministry, I can testify that the Lord's provision was never late. And, as my wife would hasten to add, it was rarely early!

Looking back, it is clear that calling Jack was one of the best decisions we ever made. He led his congregation to begin mission churches all over the area. His church ministered on numerous First Nations reserves. Jack taught with me at our Bible college, and he was a powerful prayer partner for many years. Jack's ministry provides compelling proof that the largest spiritual rewards often result from the biggest steps of faith.

HEAVEN'S BANK ACCOUNT

God's will often appears impossible to us. When God initiates a work, He bases it on heaven's bank account, not ours. It was tempting to pray for God to prompt a millionaire to bankroll our ministry so we never experienced want. But God rarely works that way. Instead, He demonstrated repeatedly that *"My grace is sufficient for you, for power is perfected in weakness"* (2 Cor. 12:10). Once God had our congregation in a position of dependence on Him, we began to experience His miraculous provision on a regular basis.

AN OPEN DOOR

As the risen Christ walked among the lampstands, He spoke words of encouragement to the congregations in Smyrna and Philadelphia. To the church at Smyrna, He declared, *"I know your tribulation and poverty, yet you are rich"* (Rev. 2:9). Though that group of believers had little money or resources, they had an unlimited line of credit with the bank of heaven! If they saw themselves as impoverished, they would behave as paupers. If they viewed themselves as children of the King, they would step out in confidence. The important factor was not how much wealth they had but how much treasure God possessed.

To the church at Philadelphia, Christ said, *"Because you have limited strength, have kept my word, and have not denied My name,*

look, I have placed before you an open door that no one is able to close"
(Rev. 3:8). That congregation faced many problems. There was a
"synagogue of Satan" in their city that was causing them grief. With
little economic, political, or legal clout, they appeared vulnerable
to those who sought to harm them. Yet Christ promised to provide
them unimpeded access to His presence. Whatever they needed
could be found in ample supply on the shelves of His storehouse. A
large donation to a church, as exciting as it may be, will be quickly
spent. Influential community members who join the church may be
transferred to another city the following year. A bylaw that favors
the church might be repealed. God's people are often mesmerized
by large donations and favorable circumstances, yet history repeatedly proves that it is foolish to place our trust in those things.
Heaven's resources, on the other hand, are inexhaustible and
entirely reliable.

The churches at Smyrna and Philadelphia were well aware of
their weaknesses, yet Christ assured them that He would personally walk with them through each challenge they faced

Conversely, the people in Laodicea were smug about their
self-sufficiency. To them Christ declared, *"Because you say, 'I'm rich;
I have become wealthy, and need nothing,' and you don't know that
you are wretched, pitiful, poor, blind, and naked"* (Rev. 3:17). That is
a strong reprimand! Laodicea was a prosperous city containing
many affluent citizens. The church was evidently ministering
without seeking God's direction or provision. As a result, they had
grown self-confident and prideful. Like so many churches today,
they focused on activity and neglected the relationship. In fact,
the church members had become so distracted that Christ had to
inform them that He was knocking on their door (Rev. 3:20).

Which church corresponds most closely to your situation?
Are you like Smyrna? Do you fret about money and paying bills?

Do you bemoan the fact that your church could do more if you had more funds? Or, like Philadelphia, are you facing threats from those seeking to harm you? Do you feel intimidated by the evil that is opposing you? Are you more like Laodicea? Have you traditionally been a self-confident church that has only recently realized how impoverished you really are?

Across America today, many established churches boast more than a century of rich history. They inherited large buildings, extensive property, and even endowments. But in many of those historic churches, the pews are empty. The nursery halls are silent. Self-sufficiency can kill a church.

Perhaps a church assumes it is healthy due to its robust bank account. It takes delight in its budget surplus but is oblivious to the paucity of people coming to Christ. Because the bills are covered, there is no need to seek God's help or ask His direction. Evangelistic events are replaced by church suppers. Business meetings are better attended than prayer gatherings.

As the congregation's focus turns increasingly inward, greater efforts are made to accommodate and appease current members. Gyms are constructed so the saints can exercise. Commercial-grade kitchens are built so the saints can eat. Comfortable fellowship halls are erected so the saints have a pleasant place to visit. As fewer people attend, greater effort is made to beautify the grounds, update the auditorium, and develop more accessible parking.

Having failed to humble themselves and seek God's direction for their church, the congregation dwindles into irrelevance. The designated youth building is empty. The beautiful auditorium is devoid of visitors. Various lots provide ample parking, but the church rents most of them out during the week to generate income.

Many congregations that were once thriving have been reduced to a remnant. Christ would say of these churches, "... *you say, 'I'm rich; I have become wealthy, and need nothing,' and you don't know that you are wretched, pitiful, poor, blind, and naked*" (Rev. 3:17). When churches like the one in Laodicea refuse to heed God's warnings, they will eventually be forced to admit the harsh reality of their spiritual poverty.

God can lead any church to a vibrant future, but they first must humble themselves and seek His direction. If they do, they will never face a need God does not meet.

TRUTHS ABOUT GOD'S PROVISION

Serving in a small church offers frequent opportunities to rely on God. You need more people, more money, more equipment, more volunteers, more leaders, and more musicians. Being continually reminded of what you lack is not necessarily a problem if you do not allow your poverty to direct your ministry. Your church's ability to minister is never limited by your resources; it is dependent on God's provision.

Before I moved to Canada, I understood intellectually that God was my provider, but it was through facing challenges that I *experienced* Him in that capacity. God invited me to serve Him in an impoverished church. Our only hope was God's supply. As a church, we learned four key truths as we experienced God meeting our needs.

I. GOD PROVIDES IN A VARIETY OF WAYS

1. God Provides Finances

God does not need to provide resources for what you are not

doing. People may say, "We will obey as soon as we have collected the required funds!" They are not acting in faith. Just as God did not stop the Jordan River until the priests' feet dipped into the water, God often waits until we start marching before He provides the resources we require (Josh. 3:15).

LEN KOSTER WALKED BY FAITH

By the time Faith Baptist Church was running 60 people in weekly attendance, God had already led us to start several mission churches. We sensed our church needed someone who could devote his full attention to traveling across our vast province looking for where God was at work. I contacted a pastor named Len Koster, someone I had met while I was a seminary student. He was a giant of a man with a huge heart for people. Our church created a new staff position, Minister of Missions, and we invited Len to join us.

Hiring him was a major step both for Len and our church. Our congregation had created a position for someone who would spend 100 percent of his time helping us give ourselves away, even though we did not yet have anyone on staff for our own youth, music, or education ministries. Conventional wisdom suggested we wait until we were bigger and financially stronger before taking such a step. But we were increasingly hearing from people across our province who told us they had been praying for years for someone to begin a church in their community. As we prayed, we clearly sensed God telling us to step out in faith and start mission churches. Most importantly, we knew that once God speaks, we must obey immediately.

Len prepared to relocate to Saskatoon. His funding came in slowly at first, and we were uncertain how God intended to provide for him. I will never forget talking with Len as he prepared to move to Saskatoon. Once again, I was asking a man to move his family, even though he was not guaranteed a regular paycheck. Len was one of the most positive people I ever knew. He told me that despite never earning a large salary, he and his wife, Ruth, had managed to accumulate $7,000 in their savings account. He said that God had given it to them, and God had a right to ask for it back. They could live off their savings until it was gone if they needed to. Then, if necessary, he would work bi-vocationally to supplement his income.

I went to my knees in prayer and wept before the Lord on Len's behalf. He and Ruth were faithful, humble servants of God. It seemed like such a high price for them to pay. Not long afterward, I received an unusual call from a man I had never met. He was a Presbyterian from another province. Somehow, he heard about Len and his new assignment with us. The man told me he believed God wanted him to send us $7,000 for Len's support. When I hung up, I returned to the Lord in prayer once more. This time I poured out my heart in gratitude. Len was prepared to sacrifice his Isaac on the altar, but God sent a ram in the thicket instead (Gen. 22:1-14).

You can imagine the encouragement that gift was to Len and to our church, but notice that God's provision came after we stepped out in obedience, not before. God did not promise to finance our good intentions. He promised to provide for our obedience.

2. God Provides Leaders

I share Len's story not just to illustrate how God provided for his financial needs but also to demonstrate the caliber of laborers the Lord thrust into His harvest in Canada.

Many churches say, "As soon as we have the money in the bank, we'll... start that mission church... call that pastor... hire a children's director..." Congregations have waited for years to do what God asked of them. They might consider their behavior financially prudent; God calls it disobedience.

I found that as we sought pastors to fill various missions positions, God often led us to successful leaders who were enjoying thriving ministries. Many took a pay cut to join us. In exchange, they were given an immense vision and the freedom to pursue God's purposes. Through the years, we enlisted outstanding leaders who experienced God in incredible ways.

When churches are small or declining, they often settle for weak leadership, because they assume stronger leaders would balk at accepting such an insignificant post. In truth, a declining church cannot afford the consequences of enlisting ineffective leaders.

Our church was keenly aware that time was short and our nation had enormous spiritual needs. We had not been called to grow a large church as a monument to our hard work. We had been invited to join Christ in building God's kingdom. Had we waited until everything was in place before we called other laborers to join us, we would still be waiting.

ROBERT CANON EXPANDED THE MINISTRY

From the outset of my time as a pastor in Saskatoon, God led our church to focus on reaching university students. As we were launching this effort, a man named Joe Rust volunteered to serve with us for two years in order to help establish our college ministry. He raised his own financial support during that time. After his two years of service concluded, we asked God how He intended to continue providing leadership for our burgeoning program.

God led us to Robert Cannon in Lubbock, Texas. He was a dynamic college minister who led one of the largest student ministries in America. Only God could compel a native Texan and his family to leave a vibrant ministry in Texas for Saskatoon, Canada! He and his wife, Corene, brought their two boys and invested their lives in our work. Robert raised much of his own financial support.

He was an organizer. Soon he was not only developing our college ministry but also helping to establish student ministries in several other cities across western Canada. Much of the growth we saw in our church was the direct result of this veteran student minister's efforts over the ensuing years. Not only had God led our church to focus on reaching university students but He also provided outstanding leadership for a ministry we could never have afforded on our own.

When a congregation is diminishing, suffering division, or facing major problems, one of its greatest needs is leadership. Yet churches in turmoil are not necessarily attractive to dynamic, visionary pastors. Here are a few things to keep in mind if your church needs to enlist strong leaders.

CALLING A PASTOR

The most important thing is not gathering resumes or posting advertisements but *prayer.* Pray with confidence that God will provide a shepherd. God had a purpose for your church when He established it. Trust that He will continue to work out that purpose. As the apostle Paul prayed for his beloved Philippian congregation, *"Always praying with joy for all of you in my every prayer... I am sure of this, that he who began a good work in you will carry it on to completion until the day of Christ Jesus"* (Phil. 1:4, 6). God's desire to reach your community will not be thwarted by your limited finances or your perceived inability to hire a pastor.

Understand that God may not answer your prayers in the way you expect (Is. 55:8-9). Perhaps at no other time are churches more tempted to pursue their own desires than when selecting a pastor. Churches often survey their members and ask what they would "like" in their next pastor. Of course, the key is not what people want but what God intends. Some people may fear that a new pastor will make changes they dislike or discontinue their favorite programs. As a result, struggling congregations waste valuable time looking for what they want rather than welcoming the pastor God knows they need.

In order to recognize God's provision, churches must keep a few important truths in mind. First, God is not restricted by your size. I have seen many churches make mistakes at this point. They assumed they were too small and insignificant to afford a "good" pastor, so they took what was available and chose a poor leader. Their decline accelerated. Do not be in a hurry! Having no pastor is always better than having the wrong pastor. Wait until the Lord shows you the leader He has chosen for you. God is not limited by your list of contacts or the resumes you have received. He can connect any servant in the world with your church. Assume God will give you His best and then patiently wait.

Second, God is not limited by your church's financial resources. When God motivates someone to serve, compensation is secondary. I took a major pay cut to move to Saskatoon. So did Jack, Len, Robert, and many others. We knew God was calling us, so we went.

When I served as a pastor in Saskatoon, my church paid me what it could. My salary alone was not enough, but the Lord regularly supplemented our income. We occasionally received boxes of children's clothes from people at my former church. One church bought us a new vehicle when they realized we were unable to purchase a car large enough for our family. People often brought food by our house so we could feed our five children. We gratefully received these gifts. Except, perhaps, for the time we were away from home when someone dropped off several large fish for us to eat. They left them in a snow bank outside our back door. It was snowing that evening, and by the time we returned home, the fish were hidden from sight. We never learned of that kind gift until months later when spring arrived and we discovered rotting fish in the melting snow!

Before you feel too sorry for my family, I must point out that God allowed us to *experience* God's provision in so many practical ways and we were the richer for it. We regularly thanked God around our kitchen table for His daily care for us.

My family was not the only one to experience God's loving provision. Each of the mission pastors did as well. Why did they willingly live by faith on that mission field? Because the Lord of the harvest had thrust them forth, and they knew they must obey, just as the early disciples had left everything to follow Jesus. Do all you can to provide for your pastor, but never forget that God has resources you do not! Your church *can* afford a good pastor if you seek the person God is raising up for you.

3. God Uses What Is In Our Hands

God can provide any resource necessary for obedience. He can also send leaders to equip you to carry out your divine mission. But a third, often overlooked truth is that God can use what you already have. At times, churches fixate on what they lack and fail to recognize what God has already provided.

I have always been inspired by the story of Moses. After God explained how He intended to use Moses to deliver the Israelites, Moses spouted a litany of reasons why obedience was impossible. Finally, God asked, *"What is that in your hand?"* (Ex. 4:2). Moses replied, *"A staff."* God commanded, *"Throw it on the ground"* (Ex. 4:3). God transformed the staff into a snake that was so terrifying that Moses, a veteran shepherd, fled from it. God said he would use Moses' staff to do wonders before Pharaoh. When God turned water into blood, Moses used the staff. When God parted the Red

Sea, Moses was holding the staff. When God brought water out of a rock, Moses used the staff. Moses may have already used that staff for 40 years as a shepherd, but he had no idea that it could become such a mighty instrument in God's hands. Interestingly, the staff remained ordinary until Moses cast it down. As long as Moses gripped it in his hands, it was just an everyday tool. He had to release his grip before it became anything greater.

Our church had to answer the same question God asked Moses: "What's in your hand?" What resources had God given us that He could use powerfully if they were surrendered to Him? When a church is declining, people's natural reaction is to tighten their grip on their few remaining resources. But God will only use what we have if we trust Him enough to loosen our grasp on it.

Our church discovered that we had many more divine resources in our midst than we first realized. We had perhaps the most unimpressive church building in our entire city, but it sat empty for most of the week. We decided to place it on God's altar. Soon, all manner of ministries began meeting on our campus. I was overjoyed to stop by the church building at almost any time in the day or evening and find people serving the Lord! Teenagers loved to gather in that place. Yes, those activities caused some wear and tear, but we came to see scuffed walls and stained carpet as signs of *life* on our property. For that, we were extremely grateful.

God blessed our church with a godly widow named Ivah Bates. She lived in a small house near the church. She was such a powerful prayer warrior that when I wanted to help our college students learn to pray, I would send them to visit Ivah. Often when God granted us a spiritual victory at the university, we knew Ivah had been fervently praying in the background. Her humble home became our church's prayer center.

At one point, we were trying to collect funds to make a down payment on a building for our mission in Prince Albert. We received a $2,000 gift from Ivah. She lived a modest lifestyle, and I was surprised by the size of her donation. Her daughter Evelyn, who had been a long-time missionary in India and Venezuela, told me that her mother had only $4,000 in savings, but she was so thrilled by our church's mission work that she wanted to participate. I was deeply moved by the sacrificial giving of our members. An elderly man in our church named John passed away. He had immigrated to Canada many years earlier from Eastern Europe. We learned that he had left his small house to our church in his will. It was not worth a large sum, but the funds came at a critical moment in our church's life. Throughout the years, we occasionally received great sums of money for our work from large churches and wealthy donors. But sometimes God's provision came from surprising sources within our own congregation. As our church members cast their shepherd's staff to the ground, God took those humble offerings and used them to bless His work.

As a church, we realized that one of the greatest provisions God grants us is people. We understood that Christ adds to the body as it pleases Him (1 Cor. 12:18). We assumed Christ would equip our church for whatever assignment He gave us. Over the years, God brought many talented university students who shared their creativity and skills with us. An architecture student designed our building expansion. A creative design student created our brochures, business cards, and stationary. A construction manager oversaw our building expansion. We were never surprised when we discovered that God had placed in our fellowship the exact type of person we needed to complete an assignment from God.

4. God Provides New Ministries

When I arrived in Saskatoon, I realized Faith Baptist Church had some unhealthy habits and practices. The church's methods had led it to death's door. The remaining members did not need me to produce more of the same results. They needed God to do a fresh, new work in their midst. Clearly, they did not have the answer for their problems. That is why they had prayed for God to send a pastor who would lead them into a promising future.

One of the great lies many dying churches believe is that they do not need to make any significant adjustments; they simply need a new pastor to help them continue down the same path. But godly leaders have no desire to preside over a church's funeral. Instead, they claim the promise of Isaiah 43:18-20: "*Do not remember the past events, pay no attention to things of old. Look, I am about to do something new; even now it is coming. Do you not see it? Indeed, I will make a way in the wilderness, rivers in the desert.*" As a small church, you may not be able to offer your next pastor a large salary, but you can present him with an enormous vision.

The members of Faith Baptist Church chose to embrace the new work God wanted to do through them. Our church was small, but our mission field was huge. We agreed that the vision for our church was not merely to "survive" but to reach our province, nation, and world for Christ. That vision made my heart race. What I find troubling is that many struggling churches are simply looking for a lifeboat. They are sinking and they know it, but they do not want to change their ways. They just want someone to make everything better. They love their building and their worship style. They have no intention of changing their methods, even those that have led their church to the brink of death. I can assure you that high-caliber people of God have no desire to invest their lives preserving the past. Embrace a kingdom vision, not a lifeboat vision.

Churches are always trying to fill vacancies in their existing ministries. While we worked to keep certain ministries—like our Sunday school department—fully staffed, we were aware that God might lead us to initiate new ministries. When God added a woman to our church who had a heart for people with Down syndrome, we believed God was equipping us to launch a new ministry. When God granted us parents whose son was incarcerated, we joined that couple in ministering to inmates. When a man who loved to minister in retirement homes joined our church, we gathered a group to work with him. Rather than focusing on what they lack, churches should ask God to reveal how he wishes to use the people already in their midst.

II. GOD BLESSES KINGDOM-CENTEREDNESS

Philippians 4:19 is many people's favorite verse: "*And my God will supply all your needs according to His riches in glory in Christ Jesus.*" Many Christians have claimed this verse as a promise that God will meet all their needs. Yet context is important. The apostle Paul wrote to the Philippian church:

> "*And you, Philippians, know that in the early days of the gospel, when I left Macedonia, no church shared with me in the matter of giving and receiving except you alone. For even in Thessalonica you sent gifts for my need several times... I am fully supplied, having received from Epaphroditus what you provided—a fragrant offering, a welcome sacrifice, pleasing to God*" (Phil. 4:15-16, 18).

The Philippian church was generous. After Paul left the city, they continued to send him financial support so he could plant churches in other communities. They were a fledgling congregation. They might have reasoned, "Now that Paul is gone, we need to raise funds to call a pastor for our church... We need to develop a building program... We'll need to order literature for our Sunday school..." Instead, they sent money to Paul to support his kingdom work.

Paul taught that when you invest in God's kingdom, He will ensure you always have enough. God blesses kingdom-centeredness, not self-centeredness. In Saskatoon, we determined that we would immediately invest anything God put in our hands into His kingdom. We knew that if we tried to save our life, we would lose it (Matt. 16:25). The best way to "save" our church was to give ourselves away.

At one point, the church in Prince Albert wanted to purchase a facility so the congregation would have a permanent meeting place. We were their sponsoring church, so they needed us to cosign their loan. Doing so meant we would be unable to borrow funds to expand our own facility. Some people in our congregation thought the mother church should not have to delay much-needed renovations on our own building in order to assist our daughter church in obtaining theirs. The building in Prince Albert would be nicer than our own facility. But we had a building, and they did not. We chose to be generous with our resources.

Sure enough, right when we were ready to begin our own building program, we received an unexpected check in the mail that freed us to expand our own facility. We never missed a beat. As long as our church kept giving itself away, we always had what we needed.

III. GOD BELONGS IN OUR BUDGET

After I had been in Saskatoon for several years, a church member asked me, "Why do we include God in every part of our church except the budget?" I realized he was right. Our annual church budget listed items we believed we could afford. Like most churches, we began by estimating how much money we thought we would receive during the upcoming year. Some of that money came from church members' contributions; the rest was from churches that supported our mission work. We planned for a modest increase each year. Then, when we had a financial benchmark, we itemized the expenditures until they matched our expected revenue.

The problem was that we allowed our resources to direct our actions. We realized that our approach was backwards. Instead, we began to ask God what He intended to do through our church during the coming year. In our budget, we listed every ministry God was leading us to undertake. Beside each item, we identified the anticipated shortfall. We would trust God to provide the finances we needed. Using our new approach, we budgeted more than double the amount we had received the previous year. We decided to allow God—not our budget—to determine our priorities. We did not spend more money than we had, but we followed God's lead and watched to see how He would provide. Do you know what happened? Not only did we receive financial gifts adequate for everything we sensed God telling us to do but we ended the year with a surplus.

Churches are in a precarious position when the phrase, "We can't afford to..." is uttered more often than "God is leading us to..." Churches generally appoint accountants to their finance committee. But remember, accountants are formally trained not to walk by faith. Also enlist prayer warriors and people of faith who will seek what is on God's heart and mind rather than merely budgeting for what you can afford. If your church's budget does not make your accountants worry a little, I wonder if you have truly heard from God!

IV. GOD EXPECTS US TO BE FAITHFUL IN A LITTLE

I have based my ministry on this truth: If you are faithful in a little, God will give you more (Matt. 25:21, 23). God will not hold you accountable for what you do not have, but He will make you answerable for what you did with what He gave you. What is the best way to receive more? Be faithful with what you already have. Faithfulness is key.

In the parable of the talents, the master gave one servant five talents, another three talents, and a third servant one talent. The servants with five and three talents immediately invested what they had been given. Investing is risky. It involves uncertainty. Yet those two servants knew their master well. They understood that he despised timidity and expected growth. They invested aggressively and doubled their funds. When they showed their master what they had accomplished with the resources he had given them, he declared, *"Well done, good and faithful slave! You were faithful over a few things; I will put you in charge of many things. Share your master's joy!"* (Matt. 25:21).

The servant who received one talent took the opposite approach. He feared he might lose the only talent he had. What if something unexpected happened? Better to play it safe by burying the talent and doing nothing. He focused on his fear of loss rather than on what he could gain. Ironically, in trying to save what he had, he lost it. The master declared, *"You evil, lazy slave!"* (Matt. 25:26). The little he had was removed from him. The master then declared, *"Throw this good-for-nothing slave into the outer darkness. In that place there will be weeping and gnashing of teeth"* (Matt. 25:30).

The Head of the church has entrusted something to every congregation. Each church has at least one talent. The onus is on us to invest our resources in what matters to our master. On the day of accounting, there will be no rewards for having merely preserved what we have. Instead, the heroes will be those who invested what their master gave them and earned the greatest possible return for their King.

◢ CONCLUSION

You will never make disciples of all nations if you only ever attempt what you think you can afford. That is not to say you should recklessly invest in every church-growth fad that comes along. Rather, let God set the agenda for your church and then confidently obey His commands, understanding that God can afford to accomplish whatever He leads you to do.

What will Christ find when He returns to your church?

◢ QUESTIONS FOR REFLECTION

1. How would you describe your church? Are you poor or rich? What are you basing your evaluation on?

2. Is your church facing challenges that are beyond your resources to handle? How are you trusting God for an answer?

3. Has your church been behaving like the church at Laodicea? Have you become too self-sufficient? How do you think God wants you to trust Him more?

4. Does your church tend to undertake only what you can afford or what God can afford?

5. Are you delaying obedience until you receive the necessary funds? Could God be waiting for you to move forward in faith before He provides what you need?

6. Is your church characterized by giving itself away or by clinging to what you have? What adjustments might God want your church to make?

7. How is your church seeking leaders? Are you trusting the Lord of the harvest to thrust forth the leaders you need?

8. Would God ever ask you to do something that is not in your budget?

9. What resources has God placed in your church that you are not currently utilizing?

10. Could your church be characterized as faithful in a little? If not, what adjustments must you make?

CHAPTER SIX

Christ's Pre-Eminence and His Church

GOD'S WAY, NOT OUR WAY

Business meetings are the bane of many pastors' ministry. During those gatherings, God's people often degenerate from saints into sinners! We believed that as the body of Christ, we needed to hear what the Head was saying to the members (1 Cor. 12). We welcomed input from everyone, whether they were a university student, an elderly widow, a businessperson, or a new member. We wanted to learn how to seek God's will together.

This approach worked well most of the time, but sometimes people applied secular practices to our church business meetings. One day, a businessman became agitated after the other members rejected his proposal. He warned of dire consequences if the church did not heed his advice. When people remained unconvinced, he grew angry and announced that he was going to resign from his ministry positions. With that, he stormed out of the building.

As the pastor, I recognized that much was at stake for our church. While we wanted to hear what God was saying to each person, no one, not even the pastor, had the right to bully other members into submission. God expects His people to behave with gentleness, kindness, and self-control (Gal. 5:22-23). If we wanted God to bless our efforts, we needed to behave in a Christlike manner. Anger will not build Christ's church. When the man lost his temper, he forfeited his opportunity to influence the congregation. Our goal as a church was to understand God's will so we could surrender our agenda to Him.

Christ is the Head of the church. For a congregation to be healthy, Christ must be the focal point of everything they do. When people take center stage, regardless of how sincerely they hold their beliefs, the church is in danger.

I visited the disgruntled church member in his home. I asked, "Can you say that you love God with all of your heart, mind, soul, and strength?" He seemed puzzled by the question. He told me he believed in God. He feared God. He also tried to obey God's commands. But he could not, in honesty, claim to love God. I learned that this man had suffered at the hands of an unloving, judgmental father. He viewed God in the same way he saw his father. He worked hard for God, yet he never felt God approved of him. That man learned an important lesson that day: If you are not rightly related to God, you will not interact properly with others.

I have known many churches where outspoken, domineering people bullied fellow members until they got what they wanted. Even as the church was declining into oblivion, a small contingent of autocrats were determined to have their way. As a pastor, I was determined that our church would not go down that path.

THE ALPHA AND THE OMEGA

Notice again how John described the risen Christ as he wrote to the seven churches in Asia:

"... the faithful witness, the firstborn from the dead and the ruler of the kings of the earth. To Him who loves us and has set us free from our sins by His blood, and made us a kingdom of priests to His God and Father—to Him be the glory and

dominion forever and ever. Amen. Look! He is coming with the clouds, and every eye will see Him, including those who pierced Him. And all the families of the earth will mourn over him. This is certain. Amen. 'I am the Alpha and the Omega,' says the Lord, 'the one who is, who was, and who is coming, the almighty'" (Rev. 1:5-8).

No one could have experienced a divine encounter as awesome as John's and not been immediately convinced that every ruler, power, or weapon on earth is insignificant compared to Christ. In light of the risen Christ, no king, celebrity, or tycoon could begin to compare to His glory and majesty. When the exalted Christ is present, nothing else matters. No other opinion is consequential. No one else merits praise or recognition.

When churches lose sight of the risen Christ, people act as if the church belongs to them. They seek the limelight rather than drawing attention to Christ. They criticize other members and divide the church in order to obtain what they want. They behave as if they will never have to give an account to their Lord for their actions (2 Cor. 5:10).

Now, as in the apostle John's time, only a clear view of the glorified Christ can save churches from the evil forces at work both within and without. As long as God's people keep their eyes on Him, they can overcome any obstacle or enemy. God's revelation to John provided a magnificent vision of the awesome grandeur of the Head of the church. Churches today desperately need the same reminder.

A WORD TO CHURCH LEADERS

When the risen Christ spoke to John, He had a message for the angels—or pastors—of the seven churches in Asia. Christ knew they needed a clear understanding of who held them in His hand (Rev. 1:20). Being a pastor is no easy assignment.

When I arrived in Saskatoon, I was the pastor of what was perhaps the smallest, weakest church in the city. When I attended ministerial meetings, other pastors would ask me where I served. Few of them had heard of Faith Baptist Church! Then they inevitably asked, "How many people attend on Sundays?" When I answered, they would express surprise or sympathy at my congregation's diminutive size. Moreover, my denomination was American in origin. Certain Canadian religious leaders believed we were not needed, effective, or welcome in Canada. I was snubbed on several occasions by pastors who held that view.

I might have felt intimidated or embarrassed about our tiny congregation had I not remembered who held me in His right hand. I could minister confidently, because it was not about me; it was about Christ.

Do not obsess over the size of your congregation. Instead, watch to see where Christ is working. Whether you are speaking to a great multitude or to a small group of elderly people in a retirement home, always minister with the profound awareness that eternity may be at stake for your listeners. Do not assume your worth as a minister is diminished if no one responds publicly to an invitation or altar call. Rejoice in the great work the Holy Spirit is doing in people's hearts. When your funds run out before you have paid all your bills, do not grow anxious. Eagerly anticipate the Lord's provision.

I learned that if the success of our church hinged on my ability as its pastor, we had much to worry about! When we focused on our Lord, we regularly witnessed the miraculous.

Successful churches keep Christ at their center. They embrace the attitude of John the Baptist: *"He must increase, but I must decrease"* (John 3:30). Churches must set aside their egos, agendas, and preferences in deference to Christ. It is His will, glory, and reputation that matters, not ours. Churches must give Christ pre-eminence in these three important areas.

1. God's Glory

God declared, *"I am Yahweh, that is My name; I will not give My glory to another"* (Is. 42:8). Perhaps the reason many churches are declining is because they brazenly extended their hand to touch the glory that belongs to God alone. The apostle Peter urged, *"If anyone speaks, his speech should be like the oracles of God. If anyone serves, his service should be from the strength God provides, so that in everything God may be glorified through Jesus Christ. To Him belong glory and power forever and ever. Amen"* (1 Peter 4:11). A church's highest achievement is not constructing a beautiful facility or assembling a large choir and orchestra. The measure of a church's success is the glory it brings to God.

Churches are in a dangerous position when pastors act as though the church belongs to them rather than to God. When pastors mistreat church members, they are behaving like a king rather than a servant of the King of kings. If they threaten to resign when they do not get their way, they are following their own will, not God's.

And pastors are not the only ones who are in danger of infringing on God's glory.

I know godly ministers who were fired because a handful of influential church members feared they were "losing control" of the church. It is heartbreaking to watch people callously and shamefully terminate a pastor due to fabricated charges and innuendo.

The instigators often threaten to take away the pastor's severance or other benefits if he tells others why he was dismissed or if he returns the following Sunday to say goodbye. When people use sinful practices to maintain power over the church, they invite God to judge them, not bless them.

Change often reveals un-Christlike attitudes. Church members might threaten to leave or withhold their tithe if the pews are replaced with chairs or a coffee station is placed in the lobby. At one church, 90 people walked out of a service because they disliked the change in worship style. I know several pastors who were fired when they tried to grant membership to someone from a different ethnicity. Make no mistake, Christ is fiercely opposed to any behavior in the church that dishonors Him.

Even as a church declines, the remaining members may stubbornly cling to their preferences. Though the remnant might claim to love Christ, they are self-centered. They are focused on what they like, not on what glorifies God. Their preferences dictate the church's operation.

Domineering church members are often unconcerned when no one is being baptized or when young people stop attending. They rarely reflect on the fact that there are few first-time visitors and even fewer who return. All that matters is that the church remains unchanged. They want to sing the songs they like, visit with their long-time friends, and hear sermons that affirm their attitudes. While that might make for a great country club, it is the kind of church that Christ spews from His mouth (Rev. 3:16).

A CHURCH THAT GLORIFIES CHRIST

Having an attitude of total dependence on God is crucial for any church's success. Our congregation had a distinct advantage over other churches in that regard. We were so close to death that if we did not fervently return to what mattered most, we would have nothing left on our church calendar but our funeral. We had no option other than to cry out to God.

Though we were small in number, we focused on glorifying Christ in all we did. We believed God received glory from worship when it came from a pure heart. A number of university students found Christ in our church, and we often invited them to sing special music during our worship services. Some singers dressed extremely casually. Others raised some eyebrows due to the vocabulary they used while introducing their song. A few, quite frankly, were poor singers! But their worship was heartfelt, and Christ was exalted.

I always asked people to share their testimony before I baptized them. Some of what they said was pretty raw, yet the congregation felt refreshed and encouraged by their zeal for the Lord. Our services were often informal and unscripted. Some visitors felt uncomfortable with that style and eventually moved on to more formal, liturgical churches. But a growing number of people were excited to discover how God was at work around us. The more we focused on Him, the more He was glorified.

Our determination to glorify a holy God impacted the way we dealt with sin. As a pastor, I strived never to excuse sin or call it by another name. Sometimes church members would stand before the congregation and confess their sins. After they shared, I would encourage people to gather around them and pray for them. We would make a covenant to walk with them and keep them accountable in the future. Occasionally, our entire service was devoted to helping people become reconciled with God and each other. Prayer meetings continued for hours because God was transforming lives, and people dared not leave. We never had the finest sound system, lighting, or musicians. But I often sensed that Jesus was pleased with what was happening in our church.

2. Christ's Lordship

Not only should Christ receive glory from the church but He also expects total surrender to His lordship.

Our congregation conducted votes differently than most churches. As the church moderator, I never asked, "Who is for this?" or "Who is against this?" Those questions would have sowed division. Instead, I asked, "After earnestly seeking the heart and mind of God on this matter, how many sense that the Lord is leading us to move forward at this time?" That question was God-centered, not people-centered. I was not asking what people wanted but what God thought.

If 55 percent of our members voted to proceed, we would wait. Because 45 percent of our church body had not yet clearly heard from the Lord, we were not ready to undertake His assignment. Though we sensed the direction God wanted us to take, we needed to determine if the timing was right. The key was never simply to achieve a majority vote but to bring people into a love relationship with their Lord so they recognized His voice and were prepared to obey.

Some pastors struggle to accept that the Holy Spirit can guide laypeople to a correct conclusion. Pastors have told me, "Henry, my people do not have the spiritual maturity to make important decisions." Of course, that is an indictment on the pastor, not the people. It is the pastor's responsibility to bring his flock into maturity in Christ (Col. 1:28). By expecting people simply to do as they are told, the pastor robs them of key opportunities for spiritual growth. More importantly, by excercising total control over the decision-making process, the pastor is behaving like the head of the church, a position that belongs to Christ alone.

Sometimes when I speak to a group of pastors, I facetiously ask, "Based on I Corinthians 12, what part of the body are you?" That question makes many pastors squirm! They know Christ is the Head, but they view themselves as the de facto head. Many pastors have never considered that they might be a knee or an eye in the body of Christ.

Our church took Christ's lordship seriously. As a result, we attempted things that seemed ludicrous for a congregation of our size. We believed Christ had the right to ask us to do whatever He chose. Jesus said, *"If anyone serves Me, he must follow Me. Where I am, there My servant also will be. If anyone serves Me, the Father will honor him"* (John 12:26). We believed that when Christ showed us where He was working, it was our responsibility to join Him.

A man who lived in the village of Leroy attended one of our church services. After he discovered that we had started mission churches across the province, he asked us to begin a work in his town too.

At one of the funerals I performed, I met a woman from the small town of Kyle, about 120 miles from our city. She told me she had been praying for someone to start a church in her town. When we drove to Kyle to meet with the woman, her house was filled with her neighbors. They asked us to help them begin a church. In both cases, we discovered that God was at work in those communities. We did not have to check our bank account or long-range plan. We joined Him.

Jesus taught His disciples how to pray: *"Our Father in heaven, Your name be honored as holy. Your kingdom come, Your will be done on earth as it is in heaven"* (Matt. 6:9-10). That was our prayer too.

We wanted God's name to be honored by our obedience. We prayed that His will would be done in our midst as fervently and perfectly as it was done in heaven. Our concern was not results but obedience.

Some communities were happy to have a new church; others were not. An aboriginal witch doctor confronted one of our mission pastors on Main Street in his town and placed a curse on him and the church plant. In another community, opponents of our work took out a full-page advertisement in the local paper condemning our efforts. A delegation from one denomination stopped by my office to discourage me from continuing our mission work. Fellow pastors and denominational leaders questioned my leadership, because they thought I was leading our church toward financial ruin. Nevertheless, we continued to complete the assignments God gave us, and we refused to focus on the naysayers. At the end of the day, our aim was not to appease our detractors but to please our Lord.

3. Christ's Character

We learned that it was not enough to *do* what Christ asked; we also had to *be* what Christ commanded. We needed to reflect Christ's nature to everyone we encountered.

During my early years in Saskatoon, I made a trip to the United States with my family. On Sunday, Marilynn and I took our son Richard with us to visit a famous church in our denomination. It boasted a large congregation that was steeped in history and great preaching. The church had also participated in our mission work in Canada. An usher greeted us warmly, and when he learned my name, he alerted the pastor that I was in attendance. The pastor sent word for me to join him on the platform so I could bring greetings to the church. Marilynn and Richard found a pew near the front so I could join them when I finished. Suddenly, an older woman approached Marilynn. My wife thought, "The people at this church are so friendly! Here comes someone to welcome us."

Then the woman, noticeably irritated, shared that she had sat in *that very spot* for twenty-eight years! She clearly intended for my wife and son to vacate her pew of choice. Now you have to understand, Marilynn did not survive raising five children as a pastor's wife in Canada by being a wallflower. She smiled warmly at the woman and declared, "Well I can certainly see why you sit here; it has a wonderful view!" The woman grumbled and noisily found a seat one pew back.

When the revered pastor introduced me, he spoke eloquently about the wonderful work we were doing in Canada. Then he asked for Marilynn and Richard to stand so the church could welcome them. The displaced parishioner gasped when she realized she had tried to expel her beloved pastor's special guests! We were enjoying a gorgeous auditorium, angelic music from the choir and orchestra, and powerful preaching from the pulpit. Yet we encountered self-centered behavior in the pews. I came away from that experience praying, "Lord, it doesn't matter how large our church grows or how many mission churches we start if our people don't reflect Your character!"

I taught the people in our church about Jesus' character and told them that the Holy Spirit would be working in each of their lives to help them act in like manner. Jesus said the last would be first and the first would be last (Matt. 20:27). He also explained that the greatest among us would be servants (Matt. 20:26). Jesus lovingly washed His disciples' feet as an example of how they should treat one another (John 13:13-17). To glorify Christ, our church had to resemble Him in all we did.

It was wonderful to see how our congregation expressed Christ's character. A woman in our church named Muriel suffered from a disability that confined her to a wheelchair. She spoke with great difficulty. Muriel was lonely and wanted to be with her church family, so someone would faithfully pick her up and drive her to every church event. Though she was difficult to understand, people patiently talked with her and included her in their activities. A college student did yardwork for Mrs. Clark, a widow who belonged to our church. Men in the church took fatherless boys hunting and fishing. A Ukrainian woman made mounds of delicious food to feed voracious university students. Our parishioners were not perfect, but they sought to be kind and welcoming. Non-Christians often told us that even though they did not share all our beliefs, they experienced love whenever they attended our church. Our goal was for visitors to leave our services impressed not with our building or music but with our Christ.

When we took a step of faith as a church, we involved everyone in the process (Mark 9:24). When people fell into sin, we extended grace and forgiveness, just as Christ would (John 8:1-11). When people wandered away from our fellowship, we pursued them (Matt. 18:12). We believed that God would not honor our *efforts* if He was displeased with our *character*. So in every way we could, we sought to reflect Christ.

◢ CONCLUSION

God chose to use our church for His purposes. He used us to reach many people for Christ. Dozens felt called into Christian ministry. Eventually, God led me to write *Experiencing God*. Millions of people around the world have been blessed by the story of what God did through our congregation. We could never have imagined that God would work so powerfully through a struggling little church in Canada. But we surrendered our control, our vision, our preferences, our comfort, and our opinions to Him and allowed Him to function as our Head. When He was finished, we marveled at God's goodness.

God stands ready to take full control of your church. He is not daunted by your current (or future) challenges. He knows how to make your congregation a mighty force for His kingdom. But He will not merely bless your plans; He receives glory when His will is done.

If you have not already done so, fully surrender your church to Him. Allow Him to make any adjustment necessary so you will be of maximum use to Him. Renounce any sin. Turn from any ungodly practice. Seek Him with all of your heart. Then quickly, fervently, and joyfully obey whatever He tells you to do next

I pray that the Holy Spirit has warmed your heart to the truth of Scripture as you read these pages. There is hope for your church. In fact, its best days are still to come. Let me warn you: Going with God will be costly. He will lead you to do things you may believe are impossible. He will even lead you to do things you find unappealing! But rest assured, it is always more costly not to go with God. He can do exceedingly, abundantly more in your church than you could ever imagine (Eph. 3:20). Let Him!

◢ QUESTIONS FOR REFLECTION

1. Do you think your church is bringing glory to God? Why or why not?

2. List several new ways your church might glorify God.

3. In what ways is Christ actively leading your church?

4. Does your church behave in a Christlike fashion? What are some areas for improvement? Is your church currently tolerating ungodly behavior?

5. What adjustments do you think God wants your church to make? What is stopping you from implementing those changes?

6. Are people behaving as if the church is theirs to control? If so, what steps may be necessary to address that issue?

7. Ask God to lay His intentions for your church on your heart. Write down what you sense God is saying. Then make the necessary adjustments to follow Him.

About the Authors

Dr. Henry T. Blackaby was an internationally acclaimed author and speaker. He served as a pastor in California and Canada for thirty years. He was also a Director of Missions and served his denomination as the Director for Prayer and Spiritual Awakening. He founded Blackaby Ministries International, which ministers around the world helping people experience God. Henry has written or co-authored more than fifty books, including: *Experiencing God: Knowing and Doing the Will of God, Fresh Encounter, Holiness, Experiencing the Cross, Called to Be God's Friend, Your Church Experiencing God*, and many more. His bestselling book *Experiencing God* has been used by God to bring revival to many individuals and congregations. Henry has spoken at the White House, the Pentagon, the United Nations, and in 115 countries, but his deepest desire has always been to encourage pastors and churches.

Dr. Richard Blackaby has been a pastor, a seminary president, and is currently the president of Blackaby Ministries International. He has co-authored numerous books with his father, Henry, including: *Experiencing God: Revised Edition, Spiritual Leadership: Moving People on to God's Agenda, Fresh Encounter, Hearing God's Voice, Experiencing God: Day by Day, Called to Be God's Leader: Lessons from the Life of Joshua, Being Still With God*, and *God in the Marketplace*. He also wrote *Putting a Face on Grace: Living a Life Worth Passing On, Unlimiting God, The Seasons of God, Experiencing God at Home, The Inspired Leader*, and *Rebellious Parenting*. Richard works with Christian CEOs of corporate America and speaks internationally on various topics, including spiritual leadership in the church, the home, and the marketplace. You can follow him at: Twitter/X: @richardblackaby or Facebook: Dr Richard Blackaby.

Blackaby Ministries International (www.blackaby.org) is dedicated to helping people experience God. It produces books and resources to assist Christians in the arenas of experiencing God, spiritual leadership, revival, the marketplace, and the family. There are also resources for young adults and
children. Please contact them at:

Facebook:	Blackaby Ministries International
Twitter:	@ExperiencingGod
Mobile App:	Blackaby ministries int
Website:	www.blackaby.org

Blackaby Revitalization Ministry

If you sense God wants more for your church than what you are currently experiencing, we want to help. It may well be that you have been doing everything you know to do. But that is not enough. You need to do what GOD knows you should do! You must seek Him for those answers. We can help pastors as well as church members seek a fresh word and direction from God. Let us help you experience a fresh encounter with the risen Christ so you are prepared for the great work God wants to do through your church.

Two resources that can help are the book Flickering Lamps: Christ and His Church and the Flickering Lamps DVD set. Working in conjunction with one another, these resources will help you discover God's truths for struggling, discouraged churches.

To learn more, go to www.blackaby.org/revitalization/ or email us at information@blackaby.org

Blackaby Leadership Coaching

Blackaby Ministries provides coaching-based solutions to challenges faced by ministry and marketplace leaders. We also help teams achieve the focus and harmony that God intends. To learn more, go to www.blackaby-coaching.org or email us at information@blackaby.org

Information about our three-day coach training workshop, The Dynamics of Spiritual Leadership Coaching can also be found at www.blackabycoaching.org/workshop/